The **Official DVSA Guide** to Learning to Ride

London: TSO

Written and compiled by the Learning Materials section of the Driver and Vehicle Standards Agency.

Published with the permission of the Driver and Vehicle Standards Agency on behalf of the Keeper of the Public Record.

First published 1998 as The Official DSA Guide to Compulsory Basic Training for Motorcyclists

Published 2005 as The Official DVSA Guide to Learning to Ride
Eleventh edition 2022

ISBN 978 011 554041 7

A CIP catalogue record for this book is available from the British Library.

Other titles in the Driving Skills series

The Official DVSA Guide to Riding – the essential skills
The Official DVSA Theory Test for Motorcyclists

The Official DVSA Theory Test Kit iPhone/Android App
The Official DVSA Highway Code iPhone App
The Official DVSA Hazard Perception Practice iPhone/Android App

The Official DVSA Guide to Driving – the essential skills
The Official DVSA Guide to Better Driving
The Official DVSA Theory Test for Car Drivers
The Official DVSA Guide to Learning to Drive

The Official DVSA Guide to Driving Buses and Coaches
The Official DVSA Guide to Driving Goods Vehicles
The Official DVSA Theory Test for Drivers of Large Vehicles
Driver CPC – the official DVSA guide for professional bus and coach drivers
Driver CPC – the official DVSA guide for professional goods vehicle drivers

The Official DVSA Guide to Tractor and Specialist Vehicle Driving Tests (eBook)

We're turning over a new leaf.

100% recycled
This book is printed on 100% recycled paper

Find us online

GOV.UK – Simpler, clearer, faster

GOV.UK is the best place to find government services and information for

- car drivers
- motorcyclists
- driving licences
- driving and riding tests
- towing a caravan or trailer
- medical rules
- driving and riding for a living
- online services.

Visit **www.gov.uk** and try it out.

You can also find contact details for DVSA and other motoring agencies like DVLA at **www.gov.uk**

You'll notice that links to **GOV.UK**, the UK's central government site, do not always take you to a specific page. This is because this kind of site constantly adapts to what people really search for and static links would quickly go out of date. Try it out. Simply search what you need from your preferred search site or from **www.gov.uk** and you should find what you're looking for. You can give feedback to the Government Digital Service from the website.

Message from Mark Winn, the Chief Driving Examiner

Riding a moped or motorcycle is fun and reduces traffic congestion. It gives you freedom and independence, but you have to remember how vulnerable you are on the road.

Over the years, different laws have been introduced to improve moped and motorcycle rider safety. They include the compulsory wearing of safety helmets, restrictions on the size of motorcycle that a learner can ride, and the theory test for learner riders – including the hazard perception test.

Compulsory basic training (CBT) was introduced in 1990. It's a training course, with no test or exam, which gives new riders the basic skills they need before riding unaccompanied on the road. CBT has had a really positive impact on road safety, but over the next few years we'll be looking at ways we can improve learner riders' knowledge and understanding at this stage.

Once you've done your CBT and passed the theory test, the next step towards getting your full motorcycle licence is passing the practical test modules, when you'll need to show your examiner that you can ride your motorcycle safely on the road. The riding standards we'll be looking for are explained simply, and with illustrations, in this book.

Riding is never predictable so, even after you've passed your test and have a full licence, you'll carry on learning. You'll be riding in different weather conditions and come across new hazards and traffic situations. Using the skills you've learnt and the guidance from this book, you'll be able to calmly assess each new situation and ride through it safely.

Learning to ride a motorcycle is a continuous process, and the tests are just one stage in your riding career. When you've passed your test, you should ask your trainer about the DVSA Enhanced Rider Scheme which'll help you enjoy your riding even more and stay safe on our roads.

Make it your aim to have a lifetime of safe riding.

Mark Winn

Mark Winn
Chief Driving Examiner

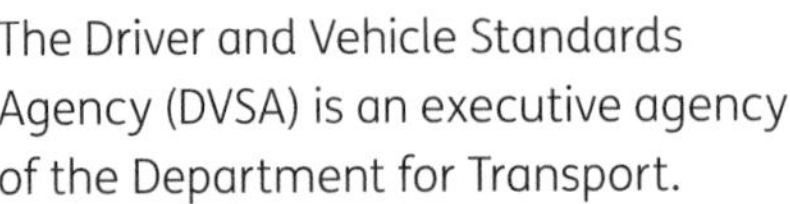

The Driver and Vehicle Standards Agency (DVSA) is an executive agency of the Department for Transport.

We improve road safety in Great Britain by setting standards for driving and motorcycling, and making sure drivers, vehicle operators and MOT garages understand and follow roadworthiness standards. We also provide a range of licensing, testing, education and enforcement services.

www.gov.uk/dvsa

The Driver and Vehicle Agency (DVA) is an executive agency within the Department of the Environment for Northern Ireland.

Its primary aim is to promote and improve road safety through the advancement of driving standards and implementation of the government's policies for improving the mechanical standards of vehicles.

nidirect.gov.uk/motoring

Contents

Introduction

Getting started

In this section, you'll learn about

- this book
- what compulsory basic training (CBT) is
- the CBT course
- approved training bodies
- your motorcycle licence.

About this book

Section 1 of this book is designed to help you get the most out of the compulsory basic training (CBT) course. Check it as you progress through each element and it'll help you gain a better understanding of what you need to achieve. The other sections will help you learn to ride competently and prepare for and pass your practical motorcycle test modules.

Important factors

You're just beginning your motorcycling career and this book is only one of the important factors in your training. Other factors you need to consider include

- finding a good trainer
- adopting a positive attitude
- patience and practice.

How you choose to develop as a motorcyclist is up to you. You should aim to be a safe and confident rider for life. Do not just put on a show for your test and then revert to a lower standard. Take pride in always setting a good example.

CBT will give you the basic skills you need to begin riding safely on the road.

Books to help you study

The official DVSA range will provide you with a sound knowledge of riding skills and safe riding practices.

'The Official DVSA Theory Test for Motorcyclists' This contains official revision theory test questions for motorcyclists, including thorough explanations of the answers.

'The Official DVSA Guide to Riding – the essential skills' This is the official reference book, giving practical advice and best practice for all riders.

'The Official Highway Code' This is essential reading for all road users. It contains the very latest rules of the road and up-to-date legislation, as well as advice on road safety and best practice. It's also available as an eBook and as an iPhone app.

'Know Your Traffic Signs' This contains the vast majority of signs and road markings that you're likely to encounter.

The information in these books will be relevant throughout your riding life, so make sure that you always have an up-to-date copy.

Ridefree

Ridefree is a free online training course for you to complete before taking your CBT course. Its aim is to prepare you for your CBT and riding on the road.

Ridefree is a combination of eLearning pre-course modules and an enhanced version of the CBT syllabus. It's based on evidence and tailored to the experiences of real learners and real trainers.

There are 5 eLearning modules that will really help you get the best out of your CBT course. They are

- Module 1 – The Highway Code and hazard perception
- Module 2 – Motorcycle clothing, equipment and maintenance
- Module 3 – The link between rider behaviour and rider safety
- Module 4A – Risk-increasing factors (part 1)
- Module 4B – Risk-increasing factors (part 2)
- Module 5 – The impact of being involved in an incident, and becoming an experienced rider.

For more information, go to

safedrivingforlife.dvsalearningzone.co.uk/ridefree/about

Study aids

The Official DVSA Theory Test Kit and Hazard Perception Kit for Motorcyclists This online eLearning platform provides everything you need to pass your motorcycle theory test. It includes all the latest revision questions and 130 interactive hazard perception clips. It also features exclusive study content and you can use it to measure how ready you are for your test.

The Official DVSA Highway Code iPhone App All the rules of the road and traffic signs at your fingertips.

The Official DVSA Hazard Perception Practice iPhone/Android App A simple and convenient way to prepare for your hazard perception test on the go. The app is compatible with Android, iPhone and iPad, and contains 30 official interactive DVSA practice clips.

You can buy official DVSA learning materials online at **safedrivingforlife.info/shop** or by calling our expert publications team on **0333 200 2401**. The team can give you advice about learning materials and how to prepare for the tests and beyond. They can also help you select suitable learning material if you have a special need; for example, if you have a learning disability or English is not your first language.

DVSA publications are also available from bookshops and online retailers. DVSA apps can be downloaded from the iOS App Store, Google Play store and Amazon Appstore and eBooks are available from your device's eBook store.

What is compulsory basic training?

To ride on public roads, you first need to get a provisional licence and then complete CBT to get a certificate.

CBT is the course that all learner motorcycle and moped riders must complete before riding on the road.

In addition, holders of a full car licence obtained by passing their driving test on or after 1 February 2001 must complete a CBT course if they wish to ride a moped using the full moped entitlement included on their driving licence.

CBT can only be given by approved training bodies (ATBs) that have trainers who have been assessed by DVSA and sites approved by DVSA for off-road training.

CBT allows you to learn

- motorcycling theory
- skills that make you safe on the road
- the correct attitude towards motorcycling

in a safe environment.

Exemption from CBT

You do not have to take CBT before riding a motorcycle if you hold a

- full moped licence obtained by passing a moped test after 1 December 1990
- full motorcycle licence for one category and wish to upgrade to another.

You'll also be exempt if you live and ride on specified offshore islands. However, if you ride across to mainland UK, you'll need to complete CBT.

Certificate of Completion

When you complete a CBT course, you'll be given a Certificate of Completion of an Approved Training Course (DL196).

The DL196 records whether CBT was completed on

- a moped or motorcycle
- a motorcycle/sidecar combination or moped that has more than 2 wheels.

This will validate your entitlement accordingly.

Certificate life CBT certificates have a two-year life. If you've not taken and passed a practical test in that time, you'll need to retake CBT.

A certificate validating full moped entitlement on a full car licence will remain valid for mopeds for the life of the licence.

Motorcycle validation If training is completed on a motorcycle/sidecar combination or on a moped that has more than 2 wheels where the 2 wheels on the same axle are more than 460 mm apart

- moped validation will be limited to mopeds with more than 2 wheels
- motorcycle validation will be limited to motorcycle/sidecar combinations.

Tests on mopeds with 3 or 4 wheels, 'A1' tricycles, 'A' tricycles and motorcycles with sidecars are only offered to riders with a disability. See table on pages 24 to 25 for information or visit **www.gov.uk**.

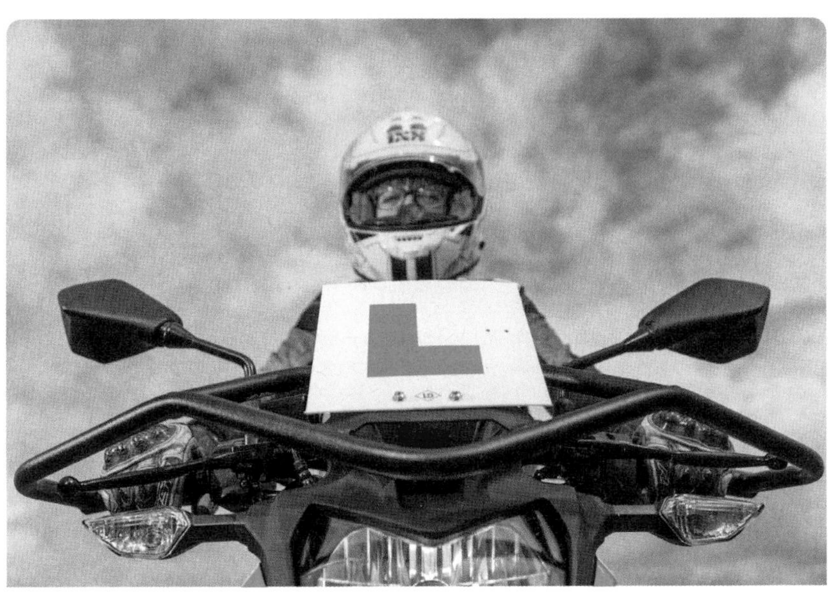

The CBT course

CBT is arranged so that you progress through a series of elements. You'll only move on to the next element when your trainer is satisfied that you've learnt the necessary theory and demonstrated the practical skills to a safe basic level.

What are the elements?

Element A – Introduction to CBT

Element B – Practical on-site training

Element C – Practical on-site riding

Element D – Practical on-road training

Element E – Practical on-road riding

The elements must be taken in this order. Each element is described in detail in section 1 (see page 28).

Within each element, the trainer is free to deliver the training in the order which they feel is most appropriate for you.

The length of time it takes you to complete the course will depend on the amount of riding experience you have, how well you've prepared and your ability to learn the practical skills to be a safe rider.

The CBT record on page 68 of this book will allow you to record when you've completed each of the elements.

For more information about CBT, visit

youtube.com/watch?v=HN2XS0gCKd8

Trainer to trainee ratios

During your CBT you may be accompanied by other learners up to a maximum ratio of

- 4:1 during on-site elements
- 2:1 during the on-road element.

For those using the direct access scheme (see page 26), the ratios are 2:1 for both on-road and off-road elements.

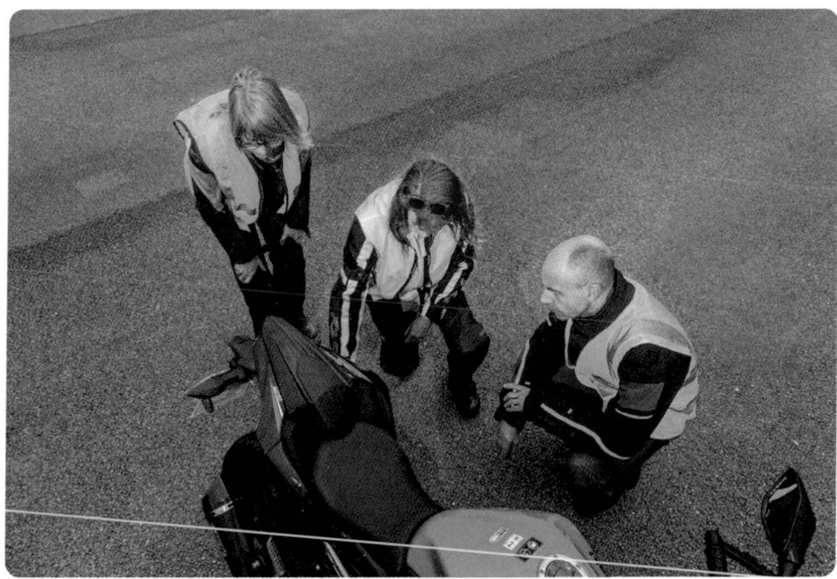

Your trainer will structure your course to suit your level of experience and ability.

Approved training bodies

Types of trainer

CBT can only be given by approved training bodies (ATBs) using trainers who are either

- DVSA-assessed certified trainers or
- down-trained certified trainers.

DVSA-assessed certified trainers Every ATB must employ at least one trainer who has successfully attended DVSA's CBT assessment. They can

- provide CBT training and issue DL196 certificates
- down-train other trainers within the ATB.

Down-trained certified trainers These trainers have been down-trained by the DVSA-assessed certified trainer and are qualified to provide CBT training, including issuing the DL196 certificate at the end of the course.

Direct and progressive access Some trainers may have a further qualification allowing them to give instruction on medium and large motorcycles. This is obtained by passing DVSA's direct access scheme assessment.

How can I tell which type of trainer is giving me training? When training, your trainer will be carrying a certificate. If it contains a 'C', they're a DVSA-assessed certified trainer, while a 'D' indicates they're direct access qualified. Some certificates contain both qualifications.

Quality control

DVSA monitors the standard of training given by trainers. If a DVSA examiner is present during your training, do not worry. The examiner will not take part in the training; they're only there to safeguard the quality of training you receive.

Choosing an ATB

You can find out about the ATBs in your area from

- the local road safety officer
- most motorcycle dealers
- motorcycle papers and magazines
- local papers or Yellow Pages
- searching online or at **www.gov.uk**
- calling DVSA on **0300 200 1122**.

Hiring a motorcycle

ATBs usually have motorcycles you can hire for your CBT, practical test or additional training.

These may be small, medium or large motorcycles, depending on your age and the licence you hold. Talk to local ATBs to find out what they can offer.

If you hire equipment and the machine from the ATB, they should provide the necessary insurance.

Clothing

Your trainer will discuss motorcycle clothing in detail as part of the CBT course.

If you're just starting to ride, ask your trainer before rushing out to buy anything, but make sure you have the right clothing to wear during your course.

During your CBT course, you

- must wear the visibility aid provided by the ATB. This will carry the name of the training organisation
- must wear appropriate clothing and stout footwear.

Many ATBs provide basic equipment for the CBT course (see Element A, pages 30 to 31).

Use your trainer's experience to make sure you get the best clothing you can for your money.

Your motorcycle licence

To begin riding a motorcycle on the road you must

- be at least 17 years old
- hold a valid CBT completion certificate
- hold a driving licence which allows you to ride motorcycles (category A).

That licence can be either of the following

- a provisional driving licence. This provides provisional car, motorcycle and moped entitlement
- a full car or moped licence. This provides provisional motorcycle entitlement.

All riders **MUST** wear a safety helmet at all times when riding (unless they're a member of the Sikh religion and wear a turban) and ensure any helmet and visor used conform to the required standards (see pages 30 to 31).

Does a non-UK driving licence entitle me to ride?

You can ride for one year from the date of entry to the UK if you hold a valid foreign licence. After this you may be required to take a test, depending on the country of origin of your licence. For further information, visit **www.gov.uk/driving-nongb-licence** or contact DVLA on **0300 790 6801**.

Do I need to request motorcycle entitlement to be added?

Provisional motorcycle entitlement is included on new driving licences.

For a list of motorcycles that can be used for practical tests, visit **www.gov.uk/government/publications/list-of-motorcycles-that-can-be-used-for-riding-tests**

Provisional motorcycle entitlement

After completing CBT, learners may ride a solo motorcycle up to 125 cc and have a power output of no more than 11 kW.

With provisional motorcycle entitlement you **MUST NOT**

- ride on motorways
- carry a pillion passenger

- ride without red L plates fitted to both front and rear of the motorcycle (in Wales you may display red D plates). If you cross from Wales into another part of the UK you **MUST** display red L plates.

What are the rules about test motorcycles?

Motorcycles with an engine size smaller than 120 cc are not acceptable for the practical motorcycle test.

Only disabled riders can use a tricycle or a motorcycle/sidecar combination for the test. (See notes below table on page 25.)

The licence obtained will be restricted to such combinations.

If you pass your test on a motorcycle with automatic or semi-automatic transmission, this will be recorded on your licence. Your full licence entitlement will be restricted to motorcycles in this category.

Full motorcycle licence

There are 3 categories of motorcycle licence: A, A1 and A2. The table below explains what you can ride and at what age.

Category	Description	Minimum age
A1	A motorcycle with a cylinder capacity not exceeding 125 cc, of a power not exceeding 11 kW (14.6 bhp) and with a power-to-weight ratio not exceeding 0.1 kW per kg	17
	A motor tricycle with a power not exceeding 15 kW	17
A2	A motorcycle of a power not exceeding 35 kW (46.6 bhp), with a power-to-weight ratio not exceeding 0.2 kW per kg and not being derived from a vehicle of more than double its power	19
A	Any motorcycle	24*
	A motor tricycle with a power exceeding 15 kW	24**

* Age 21 if you have 2 years' experience on an A2 motorcycle and you pass a further practical test.
** You can ride/drive a motor tricycle at age 21 with a full car driving licence.

Progressive access

Riders who wish to progress from category A1 to A2 or from A2 to A must pass a practical test to obtain each licence category. This test will only be available when the rider has held the licence for the lower category for at least 2 years.

Obtaining a motorcycle licence

Category A1

A full A1 licence allows you to ride motorcycles with an engine not exceeding 125 cc and with a power output of up to 11 kW (14.6 bhp). To obtain a category A1 licence, you must

- be at least 17 years old
- successfully complete a CBT course
- pass the motorcycle theory test
- pass the practical motorcycle test on a motorcycle
  - with a cubic capacity of between 120 cc and 125 cc
  - with an engine power output of up to 11 kW (14.6 bhp)
  - capable of a speed of at least 90 km/h (55 mph).

Category A2

A full A2 licence allows you to ride machines with a power output of up to 35 kW (46.6 bhp). To obtain a category A2 licence you must

- be at least 19 years old
- successfully complete a CBT course
- pass the motorcycle theory test
- pass the practical motorcycle test on a motorcycle
  - with a cubic capacity of at least 395 cc (under review at the time of going to print – please visit **www.gov.uk**)
  - with an engine power of between 20 kW and 35 kW (27 bhp to 46.6 bhp)
  - with a power-to-weight ratio not exceeding 0.2 kW/kg
  - that, if restricted, is not derived from a machine more than double its original power.

Alternatively, you can take a category A2 practical test under progressive access. If you already have an A1 licence that you've held for a minimum of 2 years, you do not need to

- take another theory test
- hold a CBT certificate.

Category A

A full category A licence gives you full entitlement to all motorcycles. You can obtain a category A licence either under progressive access, or, at age 24 and over, under the direct access scheme.

Category A under progressive access

Under progressive access, you can take a category A practical test at age 21 if you already have an A2 licence that you've held for a minimum of 2 years. You do not need to

- take another theory test
- hold a CBT certificate.

Will I have to take a theory test?

All candidates for a practical test must first pass a motorcycle theory test, unless upgrading from A1 to A2 or A2 to A under the progressive access route.

Note: If you're upgrading for any other reason, you'll need to hold a valid theory test certificate.

What defines a moped?

A moped must have an engine capacity under 50 cc and not weigh more than 250 kg.

If it was registered after 1 August 1977, its maximum design speed cannot exceed 50 km/h (about 32 mph). Mopeds built after June 2003 are restricted to 45 km/h (28 mph).

Routes to motorcycle licences

Licence category	Minimum test vehicles	Min age limit	Access requirements	
AM mopeds	Two-wheeled machine with a cubic capacity of no more than 50 cc and a maximum design speed not exceeding 45 km/h (28 mph).	16	CBT, theory and practical tests	
A1	Motorcycle without a sidecar, with a cubic capacity of at least 120 cc, no more than 125 cc, and a power output not exceeding 11 kW (14.6 bhp), capable of a speed of at least 90 km/h (55 mph).	17	CBT, theory and practical tests	
A2	Motorcycle without a sidecar, with a cubic capacity of at least 395 cc, an engine power between 20 kW (26.8 bhp) and 35 kW (46.6 bhp), and a power-to-weight ratio not exceeding 0.2 kW/kg. If restricted, not derived from a vehicle more than double its power. Note: the A2 minimum test vehicle requirements are under review at time of going to print – please visit **www.gov.uk**	19	**(Progressive access)** Held A1 licence for a minimum of 2 years – take a practical test **(Direct access)** Hold a valid CBT and theory test certificate and take a practical test.	
A	Motorcycle without a sidecar, with a cubic capacity of at least 595 cc, an engine power of at least 50 kW (67 bhp) and a minimum kerb weight of 180 kg. See **www.gov.uk** for a list of motorcycles that can be used for motorcycle riding tests.	21 24	**(Progressive access)** Held A2 licence for a minimum of 2 years – take a practical test **(Direct access)** Hold a valid CBT and theory test certificate and take a practical test.	

* Restricted motorcycles – Any switchable or variable restriction device must be installed by a reliable source and certified with documentary evidence from a main dealer, an official importer or a recognised specialist in restricting vehicles. It must be clearly evident to the examiner which power mode it is set to. An ECU or power controller that has a clearly visible, switchable power setting would be acceptable for test. Interchangeable carburettor heads/exhaust manifold restrictor or a hidden ECU would not be acceptable for multi-category testing. Any machine which is being used for multiple categories (A2 and A) must be easily recognisable as to which category it is presented for. Evidence of restriction should be in the form of a certificate or on headed paper from an official source such as a main dealer, official importer or recognised specialist in restricting vehicles and must show the vehicle registration number. You'll only need to show the certificate once unless you're using the vehicle at more than one test centre. You're advised to store a copy on the motorcycle, for example under the seat.

	Other rider information
	New riders from 19 Jan 2013 onwards – Moped entitlement will show on licence as 'AM, Q'. If you pass your car test first, you'll have the moped entitlement but will have to complete CBT to ride one on the road. **Existing riders with entitlement gained before 19 Jan 2013** – If you already have moped entitlement, you'll keep it (engine size up to 50 cc and max speed up to 50 km/h). On new/replacement licences issued to you, this will show as categories AM, P and Q. To retain your existing entitlement, P extends the AM category to include two- or three-wheeled mopeds with a higher speed of up to 50 km/h. If you already have motorcycle entitlement it will not change under the new rules.
	This licence category covers small motorcycles up to 11 kW and 125 cc, and motor tricycles with a power output not more than 15 kW. A three-wheeled moped or motorcycle is only suitable for test if the distance measured between the centre of the area of contact with the road surface of the 2 wheels is less than 460 millimetres (46 cm).
	This licence category covers medium motorcycles with a power output up to 35 kW. **DVSA will accept** • evidence from manufacturers or official importers that a specific model of motorcycle meets these requirements • an individual machine that has been restricted to comply for test as long as you show certified proof of restriction to the examiner. A dyno test certificate is not acceptable. When wishing to move up to bigger motorcycles, remember that you'll be classed as a learner on the larger machine and **MUST NOT** ride it on motorways or with a passenger until you've passed the appropriate test in that category.
	This licence category covers motorcycles of unlimited size and power, with or without sidecar, and motor tricycles with a power output of more than 15 kW. **DVSA will accept evidence from manufacturers or official importers that a specific model of motorcycle meets these requirements and will publish this information where it applies to a number of machines of a specific type. Dyno certificates are not acceptable.** When wishing to move up to bigger motorcycles, remember that you'll be classed as a learner on the larger machine and **MUST NOT** ride it on motorways until you've passed the appropriate test in that category. **B1 tricycle entitlement gained before 19 Jan 2013** – If you held category B1 entitlement (tricycles and quads) before 19 January 2013, when you renew or replace your licence it will be shown as categories B1 and A (limited to tricycles). You will not be allowed to ride any motorcycle that you previously were not entitled to ride.
	A valid theory test certificate is always required before taking the first practical motorcycle test and, unless you are taking the progressive access route, a valid theory test certificate is required before taking any subsequent practical tests on a bigger motorcycle. Tricycles – You'll need to follow the same rules if you want to ride a tricycle that falls within these categories. PLEASE NOTE that tests for mopeds with 3 or 4 wheels (see exception above), A1 tricycles, A tricycles and motorcycles with sidecars will only be offered to disabled riders. Categories A and A2 – Additional machines can be added to the list of those known to comply if there's enough evidence that they meet the new rules; this should be either a certificate or on headed paper from an official source such as the manufacturer, a main dealer or an official importer. The candidate is responsible for making sure the machine meets the new rules; if their machine does not comply, their test may be cancelled and they may lose their test fee. Different arrangements apply to candidates with a physical disability. For information and further updates, visit **www.gov.uk**

Category A under direct access

This is for riders aged 24 and over. To obtain a category A licence, you must

- successfully complete a CBT course
- pass the motorcycle theory test
- pass the practical motorcycle test on a motorcycle without a sidecar, with a cubic capacity of at least 595 cc, an engine power of at least 50 kW (67 bhp) and a minimum kerb weight of 180 kg. See **www.gov.uk** for a list of motorcycles that can be used for motorcycle riding tests.

Under direct access you can practise on any size of motorcycle that exceeds the UK learner specification provided that

- you're accompanied at all times by a qualified approved trainer, who is on another motorcycle and in radio contact with you
- fluorescent or reflective safety clothing is worn during supervision
- red L plates (D plates in Wales) are fitted and provisional licence restrictions followed.

Full licence entitlement

With a full motorcycle licence, you may

- ride without L plates (or D plates in Wales)
- carry a pillion passenger
- use motorways.

Moped riders

To ride a moped on the road, you must be at least 16 years old and have a driving licence that entitles you to ride mopeds. P is the national category; AM is the European category from 19 January 2013 (see table on pages 24 to 25). At 16 years old, this can be a full or provisional moped licence.

For 17 and over, it can also be a

- full car licence (see right)
- full motorcycle licence
- provisional driving licence. This provides provisional moped entitlement.

Remember

The same DL196 that validates your full moped entitlement will have a limited life (see 'Certificate life' on page 15) for validating provisional motorcycle entitlement.

Provisional moped entitlement After completing CBT this allows you to ride a moped. You **MUST NOT** carry a pillion passenger, ride on motorways or ride without red L plates (or D plates in Wales) fitted to both the front and the rear.

Full moped licence Full moped entitlement allows you to ride mopeds without red L plates and carry a pillion passenger.

Mopeds are not allowed on motorways, even if you hold a full licence.

Full car licence holders

Holders of a full car licence obtained by passing their driving test before 1 February 2001 hold unconditional full moped entitlement.

Holders of a full car licence obtained by passing their driving test on or after 1 February 2001, who do not already hold a full moped or motorcycle licence, **MUST** hold a valid CBT completion certificate (DL196) to validate their full moped entitlement.

If you already hold a valid DL196 when you pass your car test, the full moped entitlement will be validated immediately.

A DL196 validating full moped entitlement on a full car licence will remain valid for mopeds for the life of the licence. It's therefore particularly important to keep your DL196 safe.

Section one

Compulsory basic training

In this section, you'll learn about

- Element A – Introduction to CBT
- Element B – Practical on-site training
- Element C – Practical on-site riding
- Element D – Practical on-road training
- Element E – Practical on-road riding
- the CBT record
- further training after CBT.

Element A

Introduction to CBT

As a rider, it's your responsibility to know how the law relates to both yourself and your vehicle, so make sure that you're up to date with the rules and regulations.

This element is an introduction to CBT. It will take the form of a discussion. Your trainer will explain the basics and not get involved in complicated issues.

Wherever possible, your trainer will use examples to help demonstrate the point being made.

As a part of this element, you'll have your driving licence checked.

At the end of this module, you should understand the purpose and content of CBT. Many experienced car drivers who take up motorcycling find that CBT is an eye-opening experience which increases their awareness of hazards.

CBT overview

You cannot ride on the road until you've satisfactorily completed all the elements of CBT. Your trainer will explain the aims of CBT and will also explain why it was introduced. They should give you an overview of the course content.

Remember

Do not treat CBT as a formality you must grudgingly endure. Trainers are experienced motorcyclists who have valuable advice to give learner riders and are motorcycle enthusiasts.

Take the CBT course seriously and enjoy learning safely.

The time it takes to complete the course will be determined by you. Your trainer should not move you on to the next part until you're ready.

Within each element, trainers are free to deliver the topics in the order that they find best for you. Every topic must, however, be covered to the necessary level.

You'll need to demonstrate to your trainer that you have a basic skill level and an understanding of each topic. This may be through question and answer sessions for the theory or through practical demonstrations of your riding ability.

Equipment and clothing

Your trainer will explain the different types of motorcycle clothing available. As well as looking at outer clothing, the talk will include helmets, visors and goggles, gloves and boots.

Motorcycle clothing can be expensive and your trainer will help prioritise what you should buy first and identify less expensive alternatives. You should also discuss the effects of getting cold and wet and how some clothing can help protect from certain injuries.

Safety helmets By law, you **MUST** wear a safety helmet when riding a motorcycle on the road (members of the Sikh religion who wear a turban are exempt). All helmets sold in the UK **MUST**

- comply with British Standard BS 6658:1985 and carry the BSI kitemark
- comply with UNECE Regulation 22.05 (it will be marked with a UN 'E' mark – the first 2 digits of the approval number will be '05') or

- comply with any standard accepted by a member of the European Economic Area (EEA) state which offers a level of safety and protection equivalent to BS 6658:1985 and carry a mark equivalent to the BSI kitemark.

For the latest helmet safety standards, visit **www.gov.uk**

As well as being a good fit, your helmet must be correctly fastened.

Visors and goggles A visor or goggles are vital to protect your eyes from wind, rain, insects and road dirt. All visors and goggles **MUST**

- comply with British Standard BS 4110 Grade X, XA, YA or ZA
- display a BSI kitemark or
- comply with a European standard which offers a level of safety and protection at least equivalent to these British Standards and carry a mark equivalent to the BSI kitemark (ECE 22-05).

Goggles may comply with the EU Directive on Personal Protective Equipment and carry the 'CE' mark.

Remember

You must also know the dangers of riding

- with scratched, damaged and tinted visors or goggles (or without eye protection)
- with a damaged helmet
- without gloves or with inappropriate clothing
- without adequate clothing in bad weather.

Eyesight check

At this stage in CBT, your trainer will check your eyesight.

You **MUST** be able to read (with glasses or contact lenses, if necessary) a vehicle number plate made after 1 September 2001 from 20 metres. If glasses or corrective lenses are required to read the number plate, you must use them whenever you're riding.

Your trainer will check your eyesight by asking you to read a number plate from a set distance.

You're responsible for ensuring that your eyesight meets the minimum legal requirements every time you ride on the road. The police can stop you at any time and ask you to take an eyesight test.

What if I cannot read the number plate?

If you cannot read the number plate at the minimum distance your course cannot continue. You must demonstrate that your eyesight meets the legal minimum requirements using glasses or contact lenses if necessary, before further elements can be taken.

If you use glasses or contact lenses to enable you to read the number plate, you must wear them for the rest of the course and whenever you ride on the road.

What safety issues will I need to know about?

You'll need to understand the legal requirements for helmets and how to fasten your helmet securely. You also need to know about the BSI kitemark on visors and goggles.

How do I stop my visor from steaming up?

There are anti-fog visors available which can help reduce fogging but if you already have a standard visor you could use an anti-fog spray.

Element B

Practical on-site training

This element provides you with an introduction to the motorcycle. You will not start riding the motorcycle in this element although you'll get hands-on training.

At the end of this element, you'll be able to show a working knowledge of the machine and should have a feel for the weight and balance of a motorcycle.

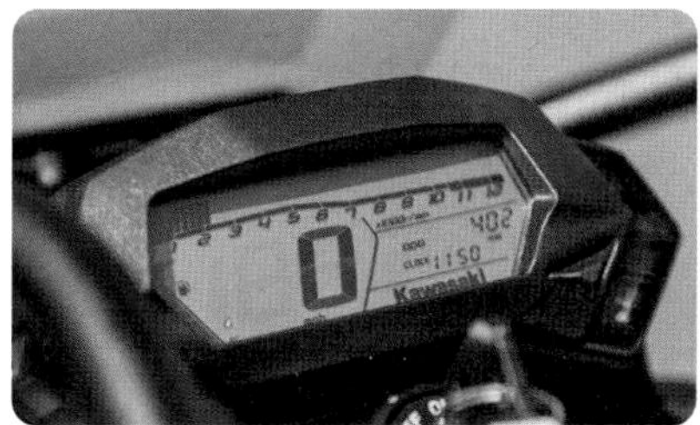

Motorcycle controls

Your trainer will make sure you know about the controls and should go through them in a logical order. The controls covered include

- **hand controls** throttle, front brake, clutch, indicators, choke, electric starter, engine cut-off or kill switch, lighting switches, horn, fuel tap
- **foot controls** rear brake, kick starter, gear change lever
- **instruments** speedometer, rev counter, warning lamps, water temperature and fuel gauges.

Basic skills Practise finding and using the controls. Some controls are adjustable. Your trainer will explain how they can be set up to suit you.

You'll also need to develop a feel for the controls.

It should not require great strength or force to operate the motorcycle's controls. Be especially careful with the throttle, clutch and brakes.

Remember

When riding you'll be wearing gloves and boots. This may affect the feel and ease with which you can reach certain controls.

You must be able to operate the controls smoothly and without having to look down to find them.

Basic safety checks and use of the stands

Your trainer will make sure you know how to make basic checks to ensure your motorcycle is safe. These checks will include the

- brakes – correct operation and adjustment
- steering – wear and adjustment
- control cables – wear, adjustment and lubrication
- fluid levels – hydraulic brake fluid, engine oil, coolant, battery electrolyte
- lights
- suspension
- wheels and spokes
- tyres – wear, damage and pressure
- drive chain – wear, lubrication and tension
- nuts and bolts for tightness
- number plate and reflectors for visibility
- mirrors for clarity.

Your trainer will also show you the types of motorcycle stands and how and when to use them.

Basic skills While you're not expected to become a motorcycle mechanic, you'll need to be able to recognise basic faults that could affect your motorcycle's roadworthiness.

When using the stands you need to

- demonstrate the correct techniques for putting a motorcycle onto and off its stands
- show an understanding of the effects of camber and gradient.

It's important that you know which machine checks you need to make on a daily basis and which can be left longer.

Make sure you're able to use the stands correctly. Incorrect methods of using the stands can lead to personal injury or damage to the machine.

Wheeling the motorcycle and braking to stop

You'll learn how to balance a motorcycle while wheeling it both to the left and right (in either order).

Your trainer will show you

- where to stand
- how to hold the motorcycle
- how to lean the motorcycle.

In addition, you'll learn how to use the front brake to stop in a controlled manner. This will involve

- making sure the motorcycle is upright
- practice to get the feel of the front brake.

Basic skills You'll have to demonstrate

- full control of the motorcycle while wheeling it
- that you have the necessary balance skills.

Your trainer will want to see that you can squeeze the front brake gently and effectively to stop.

When wheeling the motorcycle, avoid

- holding somewhere other than the handlebar grips
- wobbling
- insecure control
- looking down
- harsh use of the front brake.

Starting and stopping the engine

Your trainer will make sure you know what checks you need to make before starting the engine. A mnemonic such as FIGS may be used (see box on page 37).

Basic skills Before starting the engine you'll need to

- be able to find neutral and recognise a 'false neutral'
- demonstrate that you know how to operate the ignition switch and any immobiliser fitted
- know how to operate the starter mechanism fitted to your machine.

Before you start the engine, do not forget to turn on the fuel. If you do not, the engine may well start but will splutter and cut out before you've travelled far.

When starting the engine

- make sure you've selected neutral
- do not hold the starter button on after the engine has started.

If you're using a kick starter, do not hold the kick-start lever down after the kick over.

When stopping the engine, do not

- use the kill switch unless in an emergency
- forget to switch off the fuel tap (if fitted).

What does FIGS stand for?

Fuel You'll be shown how to

- check for fuel in the tank
- turn on the fuel tap
- use the reserve position.

Ignition The engine kill switch will be explained and you'll be shown

- the positions on the ignition switch
- how to switch on the ignition.

Gears Checking for neutral by

- checking the neutral lamp
- rocking the machine back and forward
- spinning the rear wheel on the stand.

Start You should be shown how to use

- electric starters
- kick starters.

It's important that you know how to operate a kick start but most modern bikes will have electronic starters.

Element C

Practical on-site riding

In this element, you'll begin riding a motorcycle. By the time you've finished this element, you'll have developed enough basic skills to allow you to ride a motorcycle under control.

You'll learn the essential techniques, including rear observation and the Observation – Signal – Manoeuvre (OSM) and Position – Speed – Look (PSL) routines. You'll practise until your trainer is satisfied that you'll be safe when you're taken out onto the road.

Riding in a straight line and stopping

This is the point in CBT where you begin riding a motorcycle. Your trainer will explain what you need to do, and they may also give you a demonstration.

You'll be shown how to move off and how to stop. This will include

- using the clutch
- selecting first gear
- finding the 'biting point'
- keeping your balance
- using the brakes to stop.

Your trainer will also explain about covering the rear brake and will expect you to put this into practice. They will also show you how to ride in a straight line and advise you on how to keep your balance.

Basic skills You'll need to practise until you can

- keep your balance

- co-ordinate the controls when moving off and stopping
- use both brakes in a smooth and controlled manner.

When you move off for the first time, you may feel insecure. However, from the beginning, learn to ride with your feet up on the footrests and watch the road ahead.

Remember

Never look down at the front wheel when riding. You could lose your balance.

When you stop, you'll have to put a foot down to support the motorcycle. Your trainer will explain which foot to put down. Follow their instructions and make sure you understand why.

Do not use the controls too harshly, as you could stall the engine, skid, or lose control of your steering.

Riding slowly

You'll have to show you can ride a motorcycle slowly and under full control. This is to prepare you for riding on the road, where this skill will be needed to deal with

- junctions
- slow-moving traffic in queues
- hazards.

Your trainer may demonstrate this to show the level of control you need and how slowly you'll be expected to ride.

Basic skills You'll need to

- co-ordinate the clutch, throttle and brakes
- keep your balance and steering under control.

Avoid using the throttle and brakes too harshly.

Remember

Keep your feet on the footrests. This allows you to operate the foot controls if you need to and prevents your feet from hitting anything in the road.

Using the brakes

You need to be able to operate the brakes in a controlled way so that you can

- control your speed
- stop accurately.

On the road, you need to be able to slow down and stop safely while also dealing with lose and slippery road surfaces.

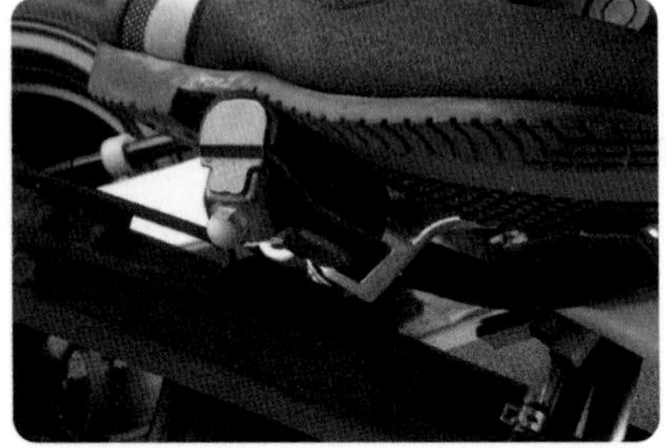

To begin with, you may find it difficult to feel how hard you're pressing the rear brake.

You'll be shown how to use both brakes together for maximum control and stopping ability. If your motorcycle has linked brakes, your instructor will explain how to use them correctly.

You'll learn to brake while your motorcycle is upright and moving straight ahead. Avoid heavy braking while turning or cornering as this can cause skidding.

Use all your fingers to operate the front brake lever. This gives you maximum control and stopping power.

Basic skills Your trainer will expect you to stop the motorcycle at a marked position. Cones, a line or some other marker may be used to identify where you're expected to stop.

Tip

Anti-lock brakes are a rider aid but, on lose or slippery surfaces, your tyres may still lose their grip.

Remember

Motorcycle boots have sturdy soles, and this can make it difficult to feel how hard you are pressing down on the rear brake.

What if I brake too hard?

If you brake too hard the affected wheel will lock up and skid. If this happens you need to release the brake momentarily and then reapply it as firmly as the conditions permit.

What are linked brakes?

Linked braking systems are where the use of one brake control activates both brakes. For maximum braking you'll still need to make proper use of both brakes together.

Changing gear

You need to be able to change up and down smoothly through the gears. This involves careful co-ordination between the clutch, throttle and gear selector.

Your trainer will explain how to use the controls to change gear smoothly. The space on the training area may limit practice to second or third gear.

Basic skills You'll need to show that you can

- co-ordinate the controls
- make upward and downward gear changes satisfactorily.

You need to know and understand how to change gear even if you're learning on an automatic machine.

Tip

Listening to the engine will help you to determine when to change gear. You'll become more familiar with this as you practise.

Riding a figure of 8

This exercise is to develop steering and balance control when changing from one lock to the other.

There are no set size measurements for this exercise. Your trainer may start off with a large layout and reduce it as your skill develops.

Basic skills You'll learn slow-speed steering and balance control, as well as where to look to help you control your direction.

You should keep your feet on the footrests and co-ordinate your use of the clutch, throttle and rear brake.

Tip

Riding in a figure of 8 gives you the chance to practise turning to both left and right at slow speeds in one manoeuvre. It will help develop your control, steering and balance.

Emergency stop

You must be able to stop safely in an emergency.

Your trainer will explain the effects of applying the brakes individually and using them together. They may also demonstrate this to you.

You need to understand

- how weight is transferred during heavy braking
- how weight transfer can affect the rear wheel
- how linked or anti-lock (ABS) brakes work and how to regain control in a skid.

Your trainer will explain how much braking effort should be applied to each wheel. The amount you should apply depends on the road surface and weather conditions.

Basic skills You must be able to co-ordinate front and rear brakes correctly and you need to avoid skidding. You can achieve this by progressively increasing the braking pressure rather than braking in a harsh and uncontrolled manner.

Rear observation

To be safe on the road, you should always be aware of the traffic around you.

You can check for traffic behind you by

- using the mirrors
- turning and looking over your shoulder.

Your trainer will explain the special requirements for a motorcyclist, including

- how and when to use mirrors
- how to overcome the blind spots.

You should practise looking round before moving off and while on the move.

Tip

If your elbows or shoulders obstruct your view behind, you may be able to fit mirrors with longer stems.

Basic skills You'll need to practise using your mirrors and looking around while moving so that you can

- see what's behind you
- check blind spots
- keep control while looking around.

Turning left and right

You need to be able to deal safely with road junctions. Your trainer will explain the OSM (Observation – Signal – Manoeuvre) and PSL (Position – Speed – Look) routines and may give a demonstration.

Your trainer will explain how to use the mirrors and the 'lifesaver' look. They'll also explain different junction types, road markings and traffic signals.

You'll need to know how to deal with left and right turns, minor to major and major to minor. A mock junction layout may be set out on the training area for practice.

Basic skills Right and left turns require different procedures. You need to

- recognise the different types of turn
- demonstrate correct road positioning
- make effective observation
- give correct signals in good time.

Tip

Do not look around when the situation ahead needs your concentration.

Remember

Make sure you cancel your signal after any manoeuvre. A signal that is not cancelled could mislead someone and lead to a hazardous situation.

U-turn

Riding a U-turn is a set exercise that also has practical use when riding on the road.

You need to be able to ride your motorcycle around in a U-turn

- under control
- with your feet on the footrests
- keeping aware of the traffic conditions.

Your trainer may demonstrate the level of balance, steering and control needed for this exercise.

You'll be given the chance to practise until you're confident.

Basic skills To ride around in a U-turn, you need to be able to co-ordinate and control your

- balance
- steering
- use of the clutch, throttle and rear brake.

You'll also need to understand when, how and where to look for traffic or other hazards, as well as where to look to help you control your direction.

The skills you gain in this exercise will be needed both in Element E and during the module 1 off-road practical motorcycle test.

Element D

Practical on-road training

Having carried out theory and practical training off-road, your trainer will now prepare you for the on-road element of CBT. The knowledge you gain now will be the foundations on which to build your motorcycling career.

This element will cover the information you need to ride legally and safely on the road.

During Element E, aspects of this theory may be reinforced in practical situations.

Conspicuity

It's vitally important to understand why you need to be conspicuous when riding a motorcycle.

Your trainer will discuss why you may not be seen and how you can make it easier for others to see you. The talk will include

- visibility aids
- differences between fluorescent materials and reflective materials
- use of headlights
- road positioning
- clothing
- keeping your motorcycle clean.

This may be illustrated by a short video presentation.

In addition, there will be some discussion on the legal requirements to use dipped headlights in poor visibility.

Being small, a motorcycle can be difficult to see, especially at some road junctions.

Making yourself conspicuous is not a legal requirement. However, it's in your own interest to make yourself easier to see. To do so, avoid

- wearing dull clothing
- riding a dirty motorcycle
- riding in another road user's blind area.

Legal requirements

Before you ride on the road, there are minimum legal requirements of which you **MUST** be aware.

Your trainer will explain about

- vehicle tax, insurance, MOT certificates and statutory off-road notification (SORN)
- provisional motorcycle licence entitlement
- DL196 (CBT completion certificate)
- L plates.

In addition, you need to know about general roadworthiness and the legal requirement to fasten your helmet correctly.

Make sure you have all the legal aspects in order before riding on the road. You will not always be sent a reminder when certain mandatory items need renewal or expire, such as

- MOT certificates
- DL196 certificates.

Do not get caught out through neglecting to keep everything up to date.

These services are available to make it easier to stay legal.

MOT reminder service **www.gov.uk/mot-reminder**

Tax check/SORN **www.gov.uk/check-vehicle-tax**

Insurance check **ownvehicle.askmid.com**

Vulnerability

As a motorcyclist, you're generally more vulnerable than other motorists. Your trainer will explain about the dangers of

- falling off
- collision, even at low speed
- weather conditions
- road surface conditions.

The head and limbs are the most exposed parts of your body when riding. Your trainer will tell you what steps you can take to protect yourself from injury and the effects of the weather.

Always buy the best protective equipment you can afford, but do not

- use a helmet that's damaged, second-hand, fits poorly or is unfastened
- ride without protective clothing
- ride too fast for the conditions.

Speed

You need to understand why riding at the correct speed is so important. Riding too slowly can be just as much a problem as riding too fast.

Your trainer will explain about the

- legal speed limits
- suitable use of speed
- consequences of speeding and riding too slowly.

Always ride within speed limits and your ability.

Remember

You need to develop a defensive riding style so that you can always stop

- within your range of vision
- in case a potential hazard turns into a real danger.

The Highway Code

As a road user, you should own a current copy of The Highway Code and check it often. You need to know The Highway Code or you'll find it difficult to deal with all aspects of training.

The Highway Code contains all the essential elements of road safety. Make sure you've read and understood it. Your trainer will need to be confident you know the rules before you can go out on the road.

It's essential that you keep up to date. Make sure you have a copy of The Highway Code.

Do not treat The Highway Code as a book to learn just for your tests. It contains a wealth of legislative instruction, other information and general advice which is designed to keep you safe and legal whenever you use the road.

Check it often and follow the advice and legal instructions it contains.

Anticipation

At all times, you should ride defensively and anticipate the actions of other road users.

Your trainer will explain that to anticipate you need to

- look well ahead
- plan ahead
- develop hazard awareness
- concentrate at all times.

Anticipating the actions of other road users is a vital part of defensive riding.

Remember

Anticipation is a skill that develops over time. Signs that show a lack of anticipation include late and harsh braking, being distracted and not taking road and weather conditions into account.

During discussion, your trainer will cover a variety of scenarios which illustrate the point being made.

Rear observation

You must understand that rear observation is a combination of using the mirrors and looking around.

Your trainer will explain about

- effective rear observation
- timing of rearward glances
- 'lifesaver' checks.

You may spend some time discussing the effects of looking around at the wrong moment.

Take care not to

- veer off-course while looking round
- look around too late
- look around when you should be concentrating ahead.

Road positioning

It's important that you understand where you should position yourself when riding on the road.

When passing parked vehicles you need to think about hazards, such as doors suddenly opening or oncoming traffic. Take up the correct position so that you can deal with these hazards safely.

Points that will be covered include how you should position yourself to deal with

- bends
- junctions
- road conditions
- single and dual carriageways
- hazards
- overtaking.

When you ride on the road, always concentrate and avoid

- riding in the gutter
- erratic steering and veering across your lane
- failing to return to your normal position after dealing with a hazard
- riding on the crown of the road as a normal position.

Remember

When riding around a right-hand bend, do not let yourself cross onto the opposite side of the road as your motorcycle leans.

Separation distance

You must understand the importance of leaving sufficient space when following another vehicle.

This will involve discussing the advantages of allowing plenty of space, such as

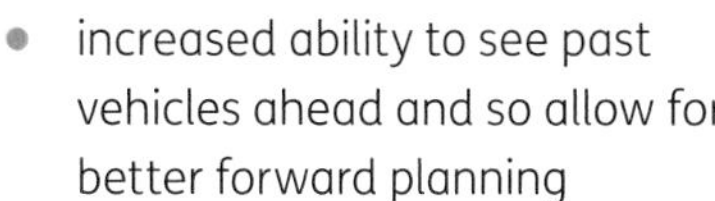

- increased ability to see past vehicles ahead and so allow for better forward planning
- increased likelihood of being seen by other road users.

Your trainer will explain the 'two-second rule' and will cover how road and weather conditions affect it.

The special advice for following large vehicles will also be discussed.

Always keep the correct separation distance from the vehicle ahead and allow for the effect that road and weather conditions have on your stopping distance. If you're too close behind a large vehicle, the driver might not be able to see you in their mirrors.

What are the usual stopping distances?

You should leave enough space between you and the vehicle in front so that you can stop safely if it suddenly slows or stops.

The safe rule is never to get closer than the overall stopping distances shown below. Do not forget that these distances will need to be doubled in wet weather and can increase up to 10 times in icy conditions.

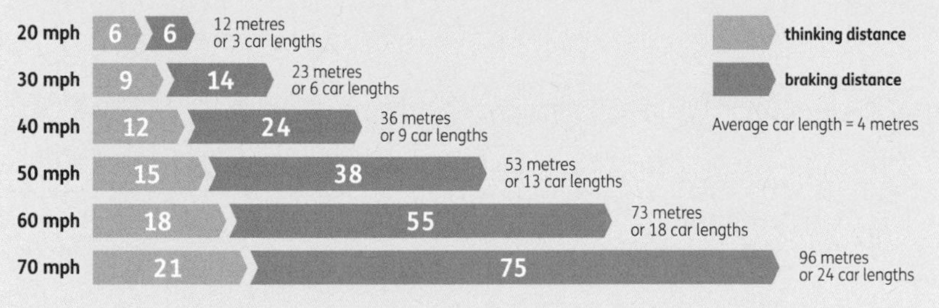

Weather conditions

Motorcyclists are affected more by weather conditions than most other road users.

You need to know how these types of weather conditions affect motorcyclists

- low sun
- wind and rain
- fog
- ice, snow and sleet.

In addition your trainer will explain how these weather conditions affect oil spillage, painted road markings and drain covers.

You need to know about the turbulence caused by large vehicles and the effect that buffeting can have on motorcyclists.

Remember

Always respect the effects that weather can have when you're riding a motorcycle.

If in doubt, do not set out.

During your training you're unlikely to encounter severe weather conditions. When you do find yourself having to ride in such conditions, remember the advice your trainer has given.

Road surfaces

You need to be aware of how road conditions can affect a motorcyclist.

A variety of road surface hazards will be explained, including

- mud and leaves
- gravel and chippings
- tram and railway lines
- studs
- road markings
- potholes or cracks
- drain covers
- shiny surfaces at junctions and roundabouts.

Clues that can help new riders will be discussed, such as

- rainbow colourings on a wet road indicating oil or fuel spillage
- 'loose chippings' road signs
- mud near farm and field entrances

Remember

When you're riding, always take the road conditions into account, especially when

- cornering
- accelerating
- braking.

Alcohol and drugs

Alcohol You're required to know that it's a criminal offence to ride with more than the legal level of alcohol in your blood. Your trainer will make it clear that despite legally accepted limits, if you want to be safe and you're going to ride, you should not drink at all.

The legal limits for riding Legal riding limits vary around the world. In England and Wales the legal limit is 80 mg of alcohol per 100 ml of blood. In Scotland the legal limit is lower: 50 mg of alcohol per 100 ml of blood. However, it's always advisable **never** to drink and ride. Even at the legal limit your concentration will be reduced and you'll be more likely to take risks.

Be aware that alcohol may remain in the body for around 24–28 hours. Your ability to react quickly may be reduced and the effects will still be evident the next morning, so you could still fail a breath test.

Your body tissues actually need up to 48 hours to recover, although your breath/blood alcohol levels may appear normal after 24 hours. The only safe limit, **ever**, is a zero limit.

Drugs Taking certain drugs when you're going to ride is a criminal offence. Many of the effects of drugs will remain in the body for up to 72 hours. Your trainer will cover

- the effect that drugs can have on concentration
- over-the-counter medicines
- how to check whether any medication will affect your riding ability
- how insurance policies could be invalidated.

Over-the-counter medicine Medicine manufacturers label their products to help you identify those that could affect your ability to ride safely. If in doubt, ask the chemist or your doctor.

Attitude

Your trainer will explain how your attitude can affect your safety. The points raised should include the

- effects of riding while angry
- importance of showing patience
- benefits of riding defensively.

Your attitude is under your control. You could put yourself at additional risk by

- riding while upset or angry
- riding in a spirit of competition on the road
- giving offence or provoking reaction by creating dangerous situations.

Hazard perception

You'll be given some idea of what's meant by a hazard.

Your trainer will explain

- the importance of planning ahead
- how early recognition makes hazards easier to deal with
- the need for concentration
- the need to use all your senses
- the importance that controlling speed has in dealing with hazards.

Remember

Always keep up to date with the constantly changing road and traffic situations by concentrating at all times and looking well ahead.

Element E

Practical on-road riding

This is the final element of the CBT course. You should only begin this part of the course when you've shown that you've learnt and understood everything you've covered on the course so far, and you can control your machine safely.

When you and your trainer are confident that you're ready, and you're not too tired, you'll ride out on the road. You'll be accompanied by a certified trainer, who will be in radio contact with you. If you're profoundly deaf, you do not need to be in radio contact with your trainer.

The time this element takes can vary for each person, so your trainer should adapt the training to suit your needs. However long it takes for you to learn to ride safely and independently, this part of the course **MUST** include on-road training that lasts for at least 2 hours. Do not worry if it takes you longer to master the basic skills of riding on the road; it will be time well spent.

When you're on the road

You'll have to demonstrate that you can cope safely with a variety of road and traffic conditions.

Expect your trainer to stop occasionally to discuss some aspect of your riding and explain how to put the theory into practice. Your ride should cover the topics discussed in this part of the book (some may not be covered because of the limits of the location).

Your trainer will constantly assess your riding. When they're satisfied that you're safe to continue learning alone, they'll issue you with a certificate of completion (DL196).

Remember, 2 hours is the minimum length of time for the on-road element. It may take longer to learn to ride safely and independently, and to be able to deal correctly with a range of hazards and different types of junction.

Traffic lights

You **MUST** know how to act at traffic lights. Apart from knowing the sequence of lights, you need to know

- what the colours mean
- how to approach green lights safely
- how to cope with filter lanes
- what to do if traffic lights fail.

You'll also need to know about school crossing warning lights.

Basic skills You must be able to

- approach traffic lights at the correct speed
- react to the road and weather conditions
- react correctly to changing lights.

Remember

If the lights are showing green, avoid any temptation to speed up to 'beat the lights'. You should be ready to stop, especially if the lights have been green for some time.

What's the sequence of the traffic lights?

Red Stop and wait at the stop line.

Red and amber Stop and wait. Do not go until green shows.

Green Go, if it's safe.

Amber Stop, unless you've already crossed the line or you're so close to it that pulling up might cause an incident.

Tip

Knowing the sequence of traffic lights can help you plan ahead.

Roundabouts

There are set procedures for dealing with roundabouts. Your trainer should discuss and demonstrate how to go left, ahead and right.

This will involve learning how to apply the OSM/PSL routine for the direction you intend to travel in. This will include

- signalling procedures
- lane discipline
- observation.

Your trainer will want to see you use the correct procedures for each roundabout you deal with.

Basic skills You must be able to

- take effective rear observation
- approach at the correct speed and judge the speed of other traffic
- give the correct signals at the right time and cancel them correctly
- follow the correct road position throughout.

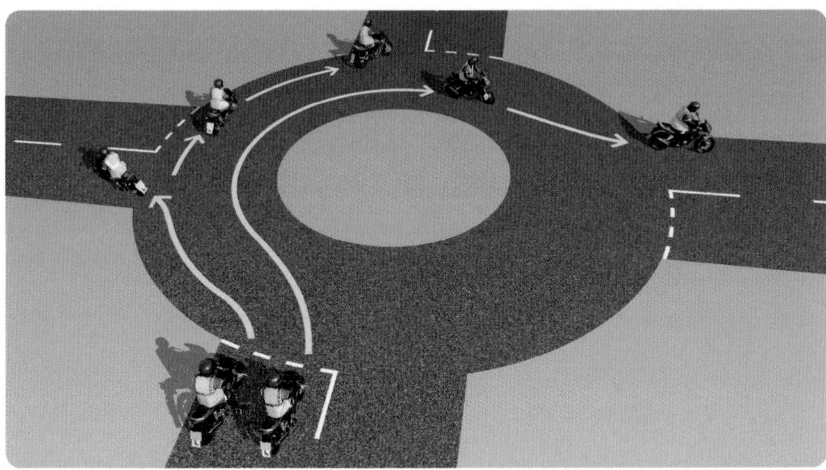

Remember

Always look well ahead for advance warning signs, especially at large or complex roundabouts. This will give you a clear picture of the layout of the roundabout, together with route directions. The sign will help you to choose the most suitable lane as you approach the roundabout.

Junctions

You'll have practised turning left and right in Element C. You'll now have to combine those riding skills with real traffic situations.

Your trainer will want to see you deal with a variety of junctions. These may include

- crossroads
- T-junctions
- staggered junctions
- Y-junctions
- box junctions.

You'll be expected to respond to signs such as

- warning signs
- 'stop' signs
- direction signs
- 'no entry' signs
- priority signs.

Do not forget to also take account of the road markings.

You must show that you're aware of other road users and watch for vehicles approaching, emerging or turning.

Basic skills To deal safely with junctions, you must

- use the OSM/PSL routine correctly as you approach a junction
- position yourself correctly on the road
- control your speed to suit the road, weather and traffic conditions
- obey road signs and markings
- react correctly to other road users
- demonstrate effective observation.

Remember

The road surface at junctions is often slippery. Do not brake fiercely or accelerate harshly.

Treat all junctions with great care.

Your trainer will make sure you can deal safely with all types of junctions.

Pedestrian crossings

There are several different types of pedestrian crossings. Your trainer will want to see you deal with crossings in the appropriate way

- **zebra crossings** slow down and be prepared to stop for waiting pedestrians
- **parallel crossings** give cyclists the same priority that you give to pedestrians
- **pelican and puffin crossings** always stop if the red light shows. You should also give way to pedestrians on a pelican crossing when the amber lights are flashing

Zebra crossings have beacons to help you see the crossing from a distance.

- **toucan crossings** do not forget to give way to cyclists on a toucan crossing, as you would to pedestrians

- **equestrian crossings** loud noises such as a horn or an engine revving can startle a horse. Switch off your engine if you think it would help the rider to cross safely.

Basic skills As you approach a crossing, you need to

- control your speed
- react correctly to people waiting to cross.

Pelican, puffin, toucan and equestrian crossings are activated when someone pushes the button.

Remember

Keep crossings clear when you're riding in queuing traffic.

Gradients

During this element, your trainer will want to see that you can cope with gradients.

This will include

- hill-start procedures
- riding uphill
- riding downhill.

You should have some understanding of how riding uphill or downhill can affect control of your motorcycle.

Remember

When riding up a steep hill, you need to be able to match the gear to the speed and load on the engine.

Basic skills To move off on an uphill gradient, you need to have good control of the clutch and throttle.

When riding down a steep hill, you need to know how to control your speed using the brakes and gears.

Tip

Steeper gradients have warning signs that show how steep the hill is and which way it slopes.

Bends

Bends vary from gentle curves to very sharp changes of direction. You must be able to recognise how sharp the bend is and deal with it safely.

Your trainer will want to see that you ride at a speed such that you can stop within the distance you can see to be clear. They will also want to see that you can keep to the correct road position. You should also show awareness of road surface hazards, such as drain covers, loose surfaces and adverse camber.

On left-hand bends, you'll have less view ahead. Be prepared for pedestrians, stopped or broken-down vehicles, cyclists and stationary vehicles waiting to turn right.

You should know how the weather affects the road surface and how that affects your safety.

Basic skills To help you assess any bend, you should be looking out for road signs, road markings and chevrons.

When approaching a bend, you need to control your speed and select the correct gear, while leaving a safe gap between you and other vehicles. You must also be able to lean into a bend while steering a steady course.

Your trainer will give you guidance to help you position correctly for right and left bends.

Remember

Your speed, position and gear should be correct before you enter the bend.

Obstructions

Obstructions are another hazard that you'll need to deal with safely.

Your trainer will want to see that you're riding defensively. That means always riding

- at the correct speed for the road, weather and traffic conditions
- in the correct position
- in the correct gear
- looking ahead, anticipating and preparing for changing situations.

Basic skills How well you cope with an obstruction depends largely on how well you plan ahead.

To cope with hazards, you need to be

- looking well ahead
- giving yourself time and space to react
- using the OSM/PSL routine
- in the correct position
- in full control of your speed.

Your attitude can affect how easily you learn these skills.

Give way to oncoming traffic if there is an obstruction, like a parked car, on your side of the road.

Remember

The way to deal with any obstruction is to look and plan well ahead, and to use the OSM/PSL routine.

U-turn

As part of Element C, you practised riding a U-turn on the training area. During this element, you'll be expected to ride a U-turn on the road. This builds on the skills you learned earlier and helps prepare you for your module 1 off-road practical motorcycle test.

Your trainer will find a quiet side road and explain what you need to do.

Basic skills You'll need to show that you have a good awareness of your surroundings and can make sure it's safe to ride across the road. You should be able to show good balance and that you're skilled in the use of the clutch, throttle, rear brake and steering.

You'll have to develop these skills to include coping with

- the camber of the road
- the possibility of passing traffic
- kerbs on either side.

Emergency stop

You've learnt and practised this exercise in Element C. In this element, you'll repeat the exercise but in an on-road situation.

This will help ensure your safety if you do encounter an emergency.

Your trainer will find a quiet side road and explain the signal to be used. You'll then be expected to ride at normal speed before being given the signal to stop. Your trainer will not let you ride off out of sight during this exercise.

Basic skills You'll need to prove that you can do all of the following safely

- react quickly to the 'stop' signal
- use both brakes effectively
- stay in control of your motorcycle.

CBT record

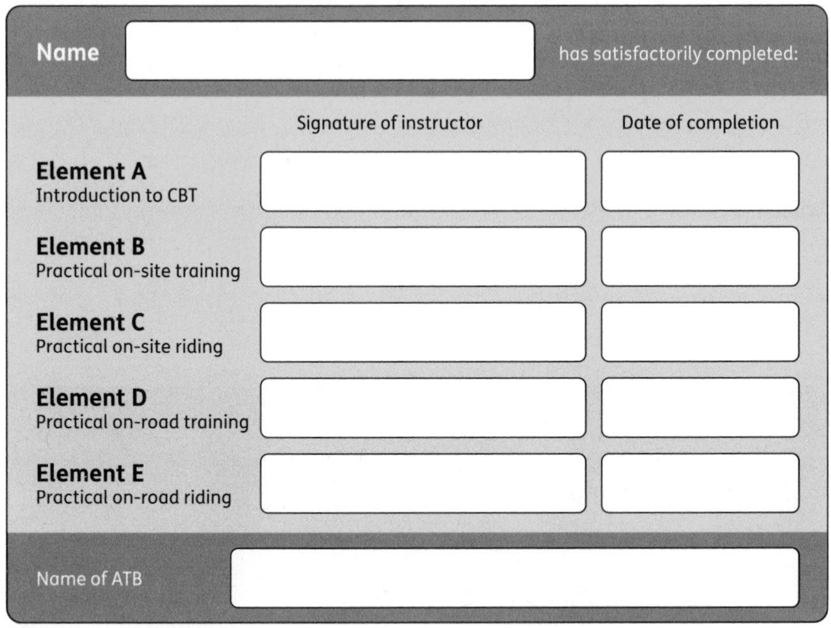

Name ______ has satisfactorily completed:

	Signature of instructor	Date of completion
Element A Introduction to CBT		
Element B Practical on-site training		
Element C Practical on-site riding		
Element D Practical on-road training		
Element E Practical on-road riding		

Name of ATB ______

Using the record

You can use this log to record your progress through CBT. As you successfully complete each element, get your trainer to sign this progress record.

This will give you

- a record of when you successfully complete each element
- a record of your trainer
- evidence of your progress to date.

Remember, you should only move on to the next element when you've successfully completed the previous one. Your on-road training must be for at least 2 hours, although it might take longer.

After CBT

CBT will give you the foundations on which to build a safe motorcycling career. However, you'll need training and practice to become good at these new skills. For this reason, you're strongly advised to take further training after you've successfully completed your CBT. Speak to your trainer for the best advice on the training you need.

Training

Many approved training bodies (ATBs) provide additional training up to practical test standard. When you attend this training, you may find that you're in a group with other learners.

There's a maximum ratio of 4 learners to each trainer for post-CBT training using learner machines.

Sometimes ATBs can book your theory and practical tests for you. Ask your trainer about further training.

Practice

This is essential. Make sure you practise

- on as many types of road as you can
- on dual carriageways where the national speed limit applies
- in all sorts of conditions (even in darkness).

In busy urban conditions, you may have to consider many hazards close together. Prioritising hazards is a skill that develops with practice.

You'll be asked to ride on a variety of road types during the on-road test module. Do not just concentrate on roads near the test centre or the exercises included in the tests. When you practise, try not to

- obstruct other traffic. Most drivers are tolerant of learners, but do not try their patience too much
- annoy local residents; for example, by repeatedly practising emergency stops in quiet residential streets.

Rural roads present some unique hazards but concentration and good forward planning should enable you to deal with them safely.

Section two

Key skills

In this section, you'll learn about

- legal responsibilities
- safety checks
- the controls and instruments
- moving away and stopping safely
- safe positioning and lane discipline
- mirrors and rear observation
- signals
- anticipation and planning
- use of speed
- junctions
- roundabouts
- pedestrian crossings
- other traffic
- country roads
- dual carriageways
- weather conditions and road surfaces
- darkness
- fuel-efficient riding.

Legal responsibilities

As a motorcyclist, it's your responsibility to know how the law relates to both yourself and your motorcycle, so make sure that you're up to date with the rules and regulations.

You **MUST** make sure you have a licence for the category of motorcycle you're going to ride (see page 21).

When riding, you **MUST** wear an approved motorcycle safety helmet (unless you're a member of the Sikh religion and wear a turban) and ensure any visor used conforms to the required standards.

To make sure you're in a fit condition to ride safely, you need to know about

- **health** – certain medical conditions must be reported to the Driver and Vehicle Licensing Agency (DVLA) (see **www.gov.uk** for details)
- **eyesight** – can you read a car number plate from 20 metres? If you need glasses to read it, then you **MUST** wear them when you're riding
- **drink** – do not drink alcohol and then ride your motorcycle. Even legally permitted levels of alcohol can affect your judgement, so it's better not to drink at all if you're going to ride your motorcycle
- **drugs** – never take drugs before riding a motorcycle; the effects can be more severe than those caused by alcohol. Be aware that some over-the-counter drugs can make you drowsy
- **tiredness** – if you're tired, you're more likely to make a mistake and this may lead to a collision. On a long journey, have a break every 2 hours or so
- **mobile phones** – it's illegal to use a hand-held phone while riding. Even a hands-free phone can distract you, making you more vulnerable.

To make sure the motorcycle you're riding complies with the regulations, it **MUST** be

- taxed and have an MOT certificate if it needs one (see **www.gov.uk** for details)
- insured for you to ride
- in a roadworthy condition.

While you're learning to ride a motorcycle, you **MUST** make sure that red L plates are clearly displayed on the front and back of the machine (red D plates can be used in Wales). You can buy these from the Safe Driving for Life website at **safedrivingforlife.info/shop/product/official-dvsa-magnetic-l-plates**.

Tips from the experts

Make sure that you know what to do if you're involved in a road traffic incident. As well as dealing with the scene of the incident, you may need to report it to the police.

HC r281–287

What to expect on your motorcycle test

You'll be asked about legal responsibilities during your theory test.

You'll need to show your driving licence, CBT certificate and theory test pass certificate when you attend for your practical motorcycle test. You'll need to show your module 1 pass certificate and pass the eyesight test as part of your module 2 on-road practical test.

Recap questions

Q1 Do L plates (D plates in Wales) need to be fitted to the front of your motorcycle while you're riding as a learner?

Q2 What's the first thing you should do if you're involved in a road traffic incident?

Reflection

Do you know about the New Drivers Act? How would you feel if you were caught breaking the law and had your motorcycle licence revoked?

Safety checks

It's important that your motorcycle is in good working order before you start riding it. You need to be aware of what to check, how to do it and how often to do it. This includes

- **Engine** – oil and coolant – check the levels are not low
- **Electrics** – check the battery, charging system, lights, indicators and horn are all working properly. Make sure the lights and reflectors are also clean
- **Brakes** – check the brakes are working properly and there's enough brake fluid in the reservoir(s)
- **Suspension and steering** – check for wear in the steering and suspension units
- **Drive chain (where fitted)** – check the chain is correctly tensioned and lubricated
- **Tyres** – check and adjust the air pressure in the tyres and check tyre tread depth and tyre condition
- **Fuel** – check whether you have enough fuel for your journey and, if necessary, plan where you can refuel.

You also need to know about the service intervals for your motorcycle.

Remember

Keeping your motorcycle well maintained will reduce the likelihood of it breaking down while you're out on the road.

Can I check all this myself?

You might need someone to help you check the brake lights. It's also easier and quicker to check the other lights if someone checks them while you're working the controls.

Tips from the experts

Make sure that you're familiar with the motorcycle you're using for the test, and that you can explain how you would carry out simple safety checks on it.

Check out the DVSA video about the safety questions

youtube.com/watch?v=gIUw46kkEzk

Recap question

Q1 What's the minimum depth of tread needed on a motorcycle's tyre for it to remain legal?

Reflection

Do you miss out routinely checking your motorcycle? If you do, ask yourself what would make you regret missing one of those vital checks. Did you know that running out of fuel is the single biggest cause of breakdowns on the motorway?

The controls and instruments

You need to concentrate on what's happening around you when you're riding, so operating the motorcycle's controls should become second nature.

You need to be able to operate the controls safely, smoothly and confidently without needing to look for them. In particular

Brakes You should use both front and rear brakes correctly and in good time. If linked brakes are fitted, you should know the manufacturer's recommended method of operating them.

Gears You should choose the right gear for your speed and road conditions. Change gear in good time so that you're ready for a hazard or junction.

Steering You should keep both hands on the handlebars and make sure your steering movements are steady and smooth.

Instruments and gauges You should also understand the meaning of gauges or other instruments, including the speedometer and various warning lights.

Switches Use the lights, horn and indicator switches correctly and when necessary. Make sure you cancel any signal at the right time. Forgetting to cancel a signal can mislead other road users leading to increased risk of a collision.

If you're riding a motorcycle with automatic or semi-automatic transmission Make sure that you fully understand the controls before you ride a motorcycle with automatic transmission. Remember, the lever on the left handlebar may be a brake and not a clutch lever. Using it by mistake could cause a loss of stability.

Tip

To give yourself time to use the controls smoothly, look well ahead while you're riding. The earlier you see and start to respond to a hazard, the more time you'll have to respond smoothly and safely. Riding in this way can also save you fuel.

What to expect on your module 2 test

Your examiner will want to see that you

- keep your motorcycle under full control throughout your test
- understand the instruments
- use the switches safely and in good time.

Recap question

Q1 When is it illegal to use your motorcycle's horn?

Reflection

Do you often find yourself needing to brake hard? If you do, ask yourself whether you could have predicted the need to brake and simply eased off the throttle a bit earlier? Smooth use of the controls can lead to a significant fuel saving.

Moving away and stopping safely

You have to move away and stop every time you ride and that's why it's so important to make sure that you know how to do this safely.

To do this, you need to

- be able to move away and stop safely on level ground, on a hill, at an angle and straight ahead
- use the OSM and PSL routines (see below)
- observe what's happening around you and be aware of any blind spots
- co-ordinate your use of the throttle, clutch and brakes so that you move off and slow down safely and smoothly

- be able to steer competently into and away from stopping places
- know where and when to look, what to look for and how to act safely on what you see
- be able to identify suitable stopping places
- know where and when to signal.

Observation – Signal – Manoeuvre

O - Observe the position of traffic around and behind you. In addition to using your mirrors, there will be times when you need to look around over your shoulder to check any blind spots that cannot be seen in your mirror. See Mirrors and rear observation on pages 84 to 85.

S - Signal when necessary and in good time so that others know what you intend to do.

M - A manoeuvre involves a change in position and/or speed.

Position – Speed – Look

P – **Position** your motorcycle correctly for the move you want to make.

S – Adjust your **speed** so it's appropriate for the manoeuvre.

L – Have a final **look** to check it's safe before you start to manoeuvre.

What if I do not have a clear view of the road?

If you do not have a clear view of the road ahead or behind, edge out slowly and only move off when you can see it's safe.

How do I stop if someone is following very closely?

Make sure that you signal in good time to let them know that you're going to slow down and stop. Slowing down gradually, over a long distance, will give the person behind time to respond safely.

Tips from the experts

Always use your mirrors but only signal if you need to – do not just signal automatically.

If you are going to park, stop far enough from the kerb so that you can lower the motorcycle's stand.

Check your blind spots (see Mirrors and rear observation on pages 84 to 85). Do not move away without looking and do not make anyone else stop or swerve.

Move away smoothly, in the correct gear and do not accelerate excessively.

What to expect on your module 2 test

Expect your examiner to ask you to stop at the side of the road on the level, on an uphill slope and behind a parked vehicle. You will then be asked to ride away from that position.

Every time you stop or ride away, the examiner will watch your

- use of the controls and OSM routine – do not forget to incorporate the PSL routine when you're stopping
- observation of, and safe responses to, other road users
- judgement in selecting a safe and suitable place to stop.

You may need to check your blind spot more than once when moving off from behind a parked vehicle.

Recap questions

Q1 When would you not need to signal before moving away?

Q2 What are you looking for in a safe place to stop?

Reflection

Have you ever moved away into the path of another vehicle or stopped without first checking what was behind you? If you have, ask yourself why that happened and what you could do to make sure it does not happen again.

Safe positioning and lane discipline

Make sure that you ride in the correct position for the road on which you're travelling. It's important not only for your safety but also for the safety of other road users.

You should be able to

- keep a safe position during normal riding, especially around bends
- deal safely with parked vehicles
- show good lane discipline, obeying all lane markings and direction arrows
- plan ahead, making sure that you position correctly and in good time at junctions
- take up the correct position on a one-way street.

To respond to the positions of other road users, you must understand

- how other vehicles, such as lorries and cyclists, need to position themselves
- what clearance you need to leave when passing stationary vehicles, cyclists or obstructions.

Remember

Plan ahead and make sure that you use the OSM/PSL routine in good time before you change position or move into another lane.

How much room should I give a cyclist when overtaking?

Give them plenty of room – as much room as you would give a car. They may have to move away from the kerb to avoid something you cannot see.

What if there are no markings on the road?

Position your motorcycle sensibly, even if there are no road markings. Do not ride too close to the kerb or to the centre of the road.

Tips from the experts

Keep to the left on a right-hand bend. This reduces the risk of collision with a poorly positioned oncoming vehicle.

Do not obstruct other road users by being in the wrong lane, straddling lanes or swapping lanes unnecessarily.

At roundabouts, do not cut across the path of other vehicles.

Make sure everyone around you knows where you want to go.

What to expect on your module 2 test

Your examiner will watch to make sure that you

- are using the OSM and PSL routines and acting on what you've seen
- respond to signs and road markings by selecting the correct lane in good time
- keep a safe position for the situation.

Recap questions

Q1 When should you use the right-hand lane of a dual carriageway?

Q2 A vehicle is waiting to emerge from a junction ahead on the left. How might this affect your positioning?

Q3 Why is it important to move into the correct lane as soon as you can?

Reflection

Have you ever found yourself in the wrong lane? Why was that and what could you do to prevent it happening?

Mirrors and rear observation

You must always know what's happening around you and act safely on what you see. To do this, you must know when to use your mirrors and when you need to look around to take direct rear observation. This is explained in Element C of CBT (see pages 38 to 47). For the most part, your mirrors will be the main method of checking behind while you're riding.

You must know

- how to make use of the OSM/PSL routines (see pages 79 to 80)
- why you need to use the mirrors and the importance of regular mirror checks
- how to act on what you see in your mirrors.

You should be aware that the mirrors will not show everything behind you (see page 45 in CBT Element C for more information about blind spots).

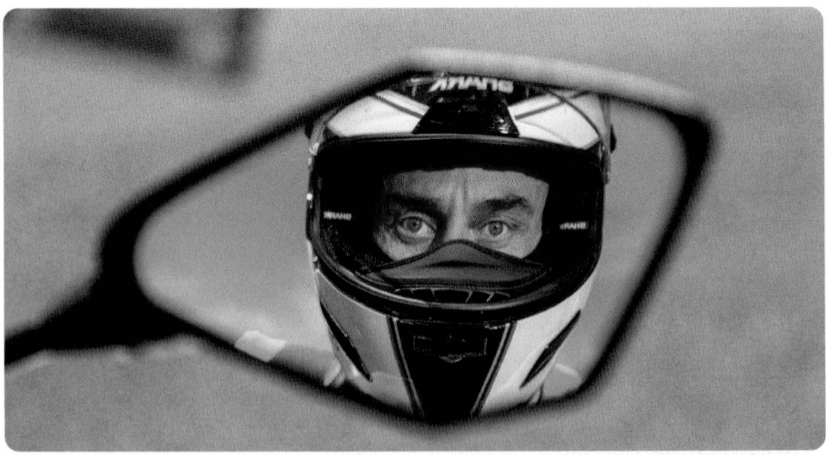

Tips from the experts

Always check your mirrors before you signal and remember that the situation may not always require a signal. Act sensibly on what you see and think about how your actions might affect other road users near you.

Use your mirrors often, especially as you approach any hazard, so that you're constantly aware of what's happening around you.

Always use your mirrors before

- moving off
- signalling
- changing direction
- turning to the left or right
- overtaking or changing lanes
- increasing speed
- slowing down or stopping.

What to expect on your module 2 test

Your examiner will watch to make sure that you're aware of the scene all around, so you need to make sure that you use your mirrors often and act safely on what you see.

Recap question

Q1 Why is it safer to use your mirrors, rather than looking around, while you're moving at speed?

Reflection

Have you ever been surprised by a vehicle that you did not see coming up behind you? Why was that? Could you do anything to make sure you're better prepared?

Signals

You need to understand, and respond safely to, signals given by other motorists and give clear, well-timed signals to other road users, including pedestrians, so that they know what you're planning to do. You should also understand all traffic signals and road markings found in The Highway Code.

You need to know

- why it's necessary to give signals – you need to signal to let others know what you intend to do
- when and how to give signals – it's important that you time your signal to allow others to respond safely
- when and how to give arm signals
- when signals are not required.

To understand signals given by other people using the road, you need to know

- the significance of other types of signal, including brake, reversing and hazard warning lights
- how to read signals given by traffic controllers, such as school crossing patrols.

Remember
You should only use signals that are shown in The Highway Code.

Should I always signal?

If you have a clear view and can see there's no-one who will benefit from your signal, there's no reason to signal.

Could I signal too early?

It could be confusing to signal too early – for example, if there are several side roads close together. Think about the situation before you give a signal.

Tips from the experts

Do not be tempted to flash your headlights for any other reason than that given in The Highway Code.

Always make sure to cancel your signal after you've carried out a manoeuvre. Leaving a signal on can lead to dangerous situations because other road users may take action based on the direction they expect you to go.

What to expect on your module 2 test

The examiner will expect well-timed signals and safe responses to signals from other people and traffic signals.

Recap questions

Q1 When can you flash your headlights?

Q2 In what kind of situation would you not have to signal?

Reflection

Have you ever failed to cancel a signal, or forgotten to give one – for example, to leave a roundabout? How does it make you feel when other people do that? What could you do to improve your signalling skills in the future?

Anticipation and planning

You should always be aware of what's going on around you while planning what you need to do in response. Planning ahead can also save you fuel, because easing off the throttle earlier means you may not need to use the brakes as often or as heavily.

You need to be able to

- use the OSM and PSL routines (see pages 79 to 80)
- identify hazards from clues and respond to them in good time
- recognise times, places and conditions that mean there's a higher risk. This includes road surface and weather conditions
- use scanning techniques to enable you to plan ahead so that you can prioritise how you'll deal with hazards you encounter.

To anticipate the actions of others, you need to be familiar with the risks associated with the various types of road user

- **pedestrians** – take special care with the very young, older people and those with disabilities. They may not have seen you and could step out suddenly
- **cyclists** – give cyclists room and take special care when you cross cycle lanes. In traffic queues, watch out for cyclists passing on your left
- **animals** – give horse riders as much room as possible and pass them slowly
- **car drivers** – be cautious as you approach a junction where a car is waiting to pull out as the car's bodywork can hide a motorcyclist from the driver's view
- **drivers of large vehicles** – they may need to take up different or unusual road positions; for example, when turning at some junctions or roundabouts
- **emergency vehicles** – do not panic; check where they're coming from and try to let them past if you can do so legally and safely.

What is a hazard?

A hazard is any situation that could involve adjusting speed or altering course. Look and plan well ahead; for example, where there are

- road junctions or roundabouts
- parked vehicles
- cyclists or horse riders
- pedestrian crossings.

By identifying the hazard in good time, you'll have the time and space to take appropriate action.

Can I use my hazard warning lights while I'm moving?

Yes, you can use them to warn other drivers of a hazard or an obstruction ahead, but only when you're riding on a motorway or unrestricted dual carriageway. On all other roads, you must use these lights only when your motorcycle is stationary.

What do I gain from anticipating and planning?

If you scan ahead, you should be able to anticipate potentially hazardous situations. By being prepared, you can deal with situations more easily, safely and in a controlled way.

Tips from the experts

You need to be constantly checking what's going on in front, behind and around you. Planning ahead reduces the risk of something happening where you have to react suddenly.

Take every opportunity to look for clues; for example, a rainbow-coloured patch on the road surface shows where the road could be slippery, or seeing a pedestrian's feet on the far side of a parked vehicle. Spotting clues can help you anticipate the hazard and take action to prevent it developing into a dangerous situation.

What to expect on your module 2 test

You'll be expected to be aware of other road users and road and weather conditions at all times. You'll also need to show an awareness of the hazards they present and respond safely and in good time.

Recap questions

Q1 What hazards could you come across on a busy residential street?

Q2 What road surface hazards might affect a motorcyclist?

Reflection

Has anything happened that caused you to react suddenly? How did this make you feel? Could you have anticipated it happening and taken action earlier? What clues did you miss?

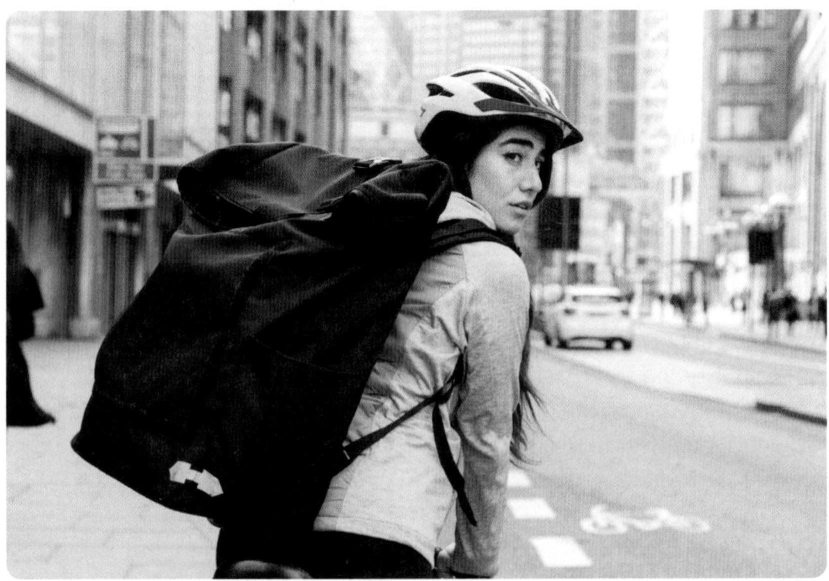

Use of speed

How fast you ride should be based on various factors, including the condition of the road, weather, traffic and other hazards. You **MUST** always keep within the speed limit.

You need to

- know the national speed limits and restrictions for different types of vehicle and any restricted speed limits for the road you're on
- adjust your speed to take account of road, weather and traffic conditions
- choose the appropriate speed where there are pedestrians and in traffic-calmed areas
- know the stopping distance for your vehicle in different conditions and how to calculate a safe separation distance between your vehicle and the one in front.

Remember

Speed limits do not mean that you have to reach that speed. Use your judgement and ride at a speed that's within the speed limit and that suits the conditions.

Can I exceed the speed limit to overtake someone?

No, you must always stay within the speed limit. It's illegal to break it, even for a short period of time.

Following behind at a safe distance

Always keep a safe distance between your vehicle and the one in front. In good conditions, leave a two-second time gap. In wet conditions, leave at least double the distance, or a four-second time gap.

To gauge a two-second gap, choose an obvious stationary point ahead, such as a road sign. When the vehicle ahead passes the object, say to yourself, 'Only a fool breaks the two-second rule.' If you reach the object before you finish saying it, you're too close to the vehicle in front and need to drop back.

Can I ride too slowly?

You should ride confidently and at a reasonable speed. If you ride too slowly or hesitate unnecessarily, it can be very frustrating for other drivers, and this can lead to risk taking and road traffic incidents.

Tips from the experts

Do not ride too fast for the road and traffic conditions and make sure that you can stop safely, well within the distance you can see to be clear. Leave extra distance for stopping on wet or slippery roads.

Do not change speed erratically or unpredictably.

Learn how to control your vehicle's speed as you approach junctions. Ride safely but avoid being over-cautious – for example, do not stop and wait unnecessarily at junctions. You should be able to move off as soon as it's safe to do so.

What to expect on your module 2 test

Your examiner will watch how you control your motorcycle's speed throughout your test.

They'll want to see that you can

- make reasonable progress along the road and respond to changing conditions
- keep up with other traffic but comply with the speed limits
- keep a safe separation distance between you and the vehicle in front
- show confidence, together with sound judgement.

Recap questions

Q1 What's the national speed limit for motorcycles on a dual carriageway?

Q2 What separation distance should you leave between you and the vehicle in front on a wet road?

Reflection

Have you ever found yourself riding faster than you realised? Excessive speed is a major factor in road incidents. How can you be more aware of and stay within speed limits?

Junctions

There are many different types of junction. You need to be able to negotiate any junction on any type of road safely, without holding up other traffic unnecessarily.

You need to deal safely and confidently with all types of junction, including

- **T-junctions and Y-junctions** – you need to make sure that you position yourself so that you get the best view of the road into which you're turning
- **crossroads** – always check who has priority as you approach a crossroads and be aware of the movement of any other traffic
- **slip roads** – these are there to help you match your speed to that of the traffic on the main road
- **unmarked junctions** – be cautious as no-one has priority here
- **junctions on all types of road** – urban and rural roads, dual carriageways and one-way streets.

You need to know the

- OSM and PSL routines (see pages 79 to 80)
- rules for turning at, entering into and emerging from a junction. These include the need to position your motorcycle correctly, adjust your speed and stop if necessary
- ways other road users turn right at crossroads and know how to adapt to different situations
- significance of advance warning signs and road markings, and acting correctly on what you see
- rules of priority, especially when dealing with unmarked junctions
- importance of good observation.

Remember

You need to look both ways when you're turning left – there may be another vehicle on your side of the road.

What if a pedestrian is crossing the road that I'm turning into?

You should be checking as you approach the turning. A pedestrian who has already started to cross has priority, so give way. Remember, they might not have seen or heard you.

How can I improve my view of the road that I'm turning into?

Sometimes buildings, hedges, bends in the road or parked cars can obscure your view. Edge forward slowly until you can see the road clearly before you pull out.

Tips from the experts

In a one-way street, move into the correct lane as soon as you can do so safely.

When approaching a junction, make sure that you slow down in good time so that you do not have to brake heavily if you need to stop.

Watch out for pedestrians, cyclists and motorcyclists when you're turning, as they're not as easy to see as larger vehicles.

What to expect on your module 2 test

Your examiner will watch carefully to take account of your

- use of the OSM and PSL routines
- position and speed as you approach junctions
- observation and judgement.

Recap questions

Q1 When can you wait on the yellow crisscross lines at a box junction?

Q2 Who has priority if there are no road markings at a crossroads?

Q3 How should you negotiate a traffic-light-controlled junction that has an advanced stop line for cyclists?

Reflection

Many collisions happen at road junctions and 'I did not see you' is often mentioned. Why do you think that is? Is there anything you could do to reduce the risk at junctions?

Positioning correctly before turning right helps other road users know which way you're going. If the road is wide enough, it also allows traffic to flow past on your left.

Roundabouts

To deal with roundabouts safely and confidently, you should have a thorough understanding of the rules that apply when approaching and negotiating them.

You need to be able to safely negotiate different types of roundabout, including

- **standard roundabouts** – you should know how to approach and negotiate roundabouts even when there are no road markings directing you into particular lanes
- **mini-roundabouts** – you'll probably need to adjust your speed on approach because there's less room to manoeuvre and less time to signal
- **multiple and satellite roundabouts** – assess the layout of the roundabouts by looking at the signs on approach. Treat each roundabout separately and apply the normal rules
- **traffic-light-controlled roundabouts** – priorities will often be different from normal roundabouts here.

You need to know

- how and when to apply the OSM and PSL routines (see pages 79 to 80)
- the importance of effective observation and awareness of the traffic around you
- how to position correctly and which lane to use, both as you approach and when you're on a roundabout
- who has priority when you're entering a roundabout
- the procedure for leaving a roundabout.

Remember

If you're behind another vehicle waiting to join a roundabout, do not move forward before checking that the vehicle in front of you has moved away. You may think it's safe to join the roundabout but they may judge the situation differently.

What if there's a long vehicle at the roundabout?

Stay well back and give it plenty of room. It might need to take a different course as it approaches and goes around the roundabout.

When should I start indicating to show I'm taking an exit?

You need to turn your left indicator on just after you've passed the exit before the one that you want to take. If your signal does not cancel automatically, cancel it manually when you've finished turning.

Tips from the experts

Approach the roundabout at the correct speed so that you can assess other traffic using the roundabout. If you need to stop, avoid braking harshly.

Roundabouts are there to help traffic move freely. Do not stop unless you need to.

Look at all the road signs and markings and make sure you get into the correct lane in good time.

What to expect on your module 2 test

Your examiner will take account of your ability to deal with roundabouts without undue hesitation. This will include your use of the OSM and PSL routines, your position, speed on approach, observation and judgement throughout.

Recap question

Q1 Why would a cyclist signal right but stay in the left-hand lane as they approach a roundabout?

Reflection

Some people find roundabouts difficult to deal with. Have you ever become confused and taken the wrong exit? How could you make sure you're better prepared?

Pedestrian crossings

You should be aware of the basic rules that apply to all pedestrian crossings but you also need to know the differences between each type of crossing.

You need to safely negotiate different types of crossing. This includes

- **crossings controlled by lights** – pelican, puffin and toucan crossings
- **zebra crossings** – which have no lights controlling them
- **parallel crossings** – where cyclists cross alongside a zebra crossing and have the same priority as pedestrians
- **school crossing patrols** – these are not always at marked crossings
- **split crossings** – this includes crossings that are staggered and those that have a central refuge.

You need to know

- the importance of effective scanning as you approach a crossing
- how to recognise the different types of crossing from their visual characteristics
- how you should apply the OSM and PSL routines (see pages 79 to 80)
- the correct speed to approach crossings and the rules concerning overtaking and parking near crossings

- when you need to stop for pedestrians who are waiting to cross
- the times and places where there's likely to be high risk; for example, near schools
- the effect that different weather conditions have on your ability to see and stop safely.

Remember

It's illegal to park on a crossing or on the zigzag lines on either side of the crossing. It's also illegal to overtake the vehicle nearest the crossing.

Can I wave to let a pedestrian know they can cross?

You should never wave pedestrians across in front of you as you could lead them into danger. Let them decide for themselves when it's safe to cross.

What should I look for when I'm approaching a crossing?

Watch out for pedestrians walking close to crossings, especially zebra crossings, as they may start to cross without looking for traffic.

Tips from the experts

Make sure that you approach all crossings at a speed that allows you to stop safely if you need to.

As you approach a zebra crossing, look for pedestrians who may be intending to use the crossing.

Be patient when you're waiting at a crossing. Do not try to hurry those who are crossing by revving your engine, sounding your horn or edging forward.

What to expect on your module 2 test

Your examiner will watch carefully to assess how you deal with pedestrian crossings during your test. This includes how you prepare on the approach to crossings even when you do not have to stop to let pedestrians cross.

Recap questions

Q1 Which type of crossing has a flashing amber phase, and what does it mean for you as a rider?

Q2 What do the zigzag lines at a crossing mean?

Reflection

Why might you fail to notice someone waiting at a zebra crossing? What could you do to raise your awareness of pedestrian crossings?

If you're waiting in a queue of traffic, do not straddle a crossing. Hold back, as someone may want to cross before you're able to move off. At a controlled crossing, the lights might change.

Other traffic

In most cases when you're riding, there will be other traffic on the road. You need to be able to deal safely and confidently when meeting, crossing and overtaking other vehicles.

You need to be able to deal with

- **meeting** – where there are parked cars or obstructions on your side of the road, you must be prepared to give way to oncoming traffic. On narrow roads, you may need to use passing places
- **crossing** – you normally need to cross the path of other traffic if you're turning right into a side road or driveway. Make sure that you position correctly, as close to the centre of the road as is safe, and watch out for oncoming traffic, stopping if necessary. Do not forget to check your mirror and blind area before turning, in case a vehicle is overtaking you when you want to turn
- **overtaking** – overtake only if you can do so legally and safely. Check the speed and position of any vehicles behind (they might be planning to overtake you), in front, and coming towards you before you decide to overtake.

You need to know

- the OSM and PSL routines (see pages 79 to 80)
- why and when to give way – you should not cause another road user to slow down or alter their course when they have priority
- the significance of passing places, warning signs, road markings and how to deal with obstructions
- the importance of planning and anticipation, and acting safely on what you see
- how to use all road types, including a one-way street, single carriageway, a three-lane single carriageway, dual carriageway and a motorway.

Remember

Do not overtake as you approach a junction. A vehicle could pull out of the junction into your path.

Can I pull out of a side road if an approaching driver is indicating to turn into the side road?

Always wait until you're sure they're turning before you move out. They may have forgotten to cancel their signal from an earlier manoeuvre.

Can I flash my lights to give someone the go-ahead?

No. The Highway Code states that you should only flash your lights as a warning, to let someone know you're there.

Tips from the experts

When passing parked cars, watch out for doors opening, pedestrians (especially children) stepping out from between the cars, and vehicles pulling out.

When overtaking cyclists or horse riders, slow down and give them as much room as you would for a car.

If you're going to pass an obstruction or overtake, start planning early so that you get a better view of the road ahead.

What to expect on your module 2 test

Your examiner will watch to see how you

- apply the OSM and PSL routines
- respond to road and traffic conditions
- control your motorcycle.

Recap questions

Q1 Give 3 examples of where it's against the law to overtake.

Q2 On a one-way street, which side can you pass traffic?

Q3 You see a large vehicle coming towards you on a narrow road. There's a passing place just ahead on the other side of the road. What should you do?

Reflection

Have you ever become frustrated while following a slow-moving vehicle? What could you do to make the delay less stressful?

Country roads

Country roads vary from trunk roads, carrying heavy traffic, to narrow lanes, where there's only room for single-file traffic. Unless signs show otherwise, the national speed limit will apply but that is the maximum speed limit – it does not indicate that it's safe to ride at that speed. You must determine the safe speed within the limit, using your judgement, while taking account of the visibility, signs, hazards and other traffic, as well as road and weather conditions.

You need to be able to deal with

- poor visibility due to bends, hedgerows and steep roadsides
- gradients and camber
- junctions and entrances
- vulnerable road users, including pedestrians, cyclists and horse riders
- slow-moving agricultural machinery
- poor road surfaces
- darkness and various weather conditions.

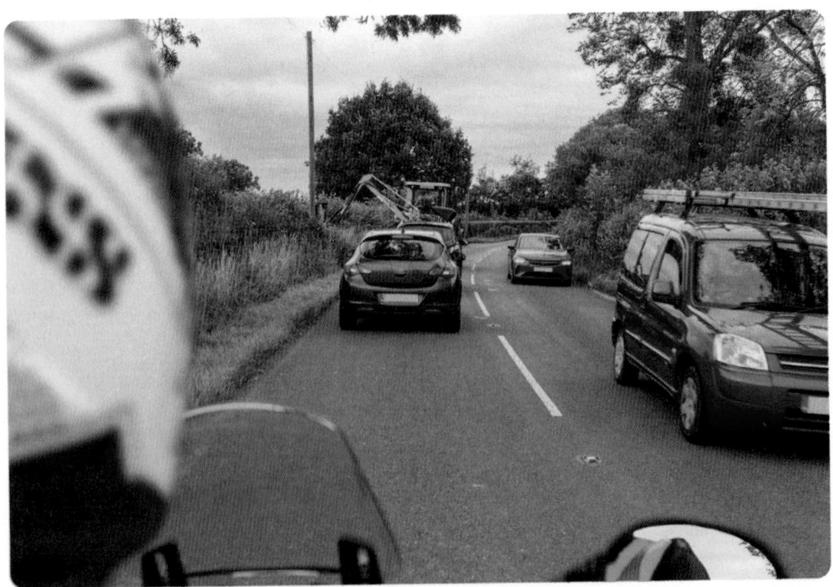

You need to know

- the OSM and PSL routines (see pages 79 to 80)
- what the different road signs mean
- the importance of forward planning
- how to scan ahead to anticipate hazards that could be out of sight
- how to use passing places.

Remember

There are often no pavements on country roads and pedestrians will be walking on the road.

Should I sound the horn if I come across livestock on the road?

Animals will probably be startled by the sound of your horn and their response may be unpredictable. Be patient and pass them slowly.

How fast should I ride?

Always ride at a speed that will allow you to stop within the distance you can see to be clear. Allow for a longer stopping distance when the road is wet or slippery.

Tips from the experts

If you come across mud on the road, it's likely that the vehicle responsible is not far away. Be prepared to find an agricultural vehicle up ahead.

When there are no pavements, pedestrians are advised to walk facing the traffic. This means they'll be on your side of the road. Have this in mind when the road bends and you cannot see what's ahead.

Country roads do not have street lighting. At night, make sure you switch your headlights to dipped beam so that you do not dazzle oncoming drivers.

Remember

Always ride slowly and quietly past horses and leave them as much room as you can.

Recap question

Q1 What hazards would you expect to find on country roads?

Reflection

Have you ever considered how your riding might be viewed by someone else? If you were in charge of a horse, walking or cycling along the road, how would you like a motorcyclist to behave? Is anything stopping you from behaving that way?

Dual carriageways

Some dual carriageways share the same speed limit as motorways and you join some dual carriageways from a slip road, in a similar way to joining a motorway. Unlike a motorway, though, dual carriageways can have junctions and roundabouts where traffic can join, leave, cross and turn right from the carriageway.

You need to be able to

- ride safely on urban and rural dual carriageways and clearways
- join a dual carriageway – if there's a slip road, use it to adjust your speed to match any vehicles on the dual carriageway and join where there's a suitable gap. If there's no slip road, join as you would on any other road
- choose the correct lane. Before leaving, you should move into the correct lane in good time
- turn right off a dual carriageway.

You need to know

- the OSM and PSL routines (see pages 79 to 80)
- the various speed limits that may be used on dual carriageways
- how to respond to advance warning and information signs
- what you should do if your motorcycle breaks down, including the use of your hazard warning lights and warning triangles
- how the weather can affect you while you're riding on a dual carriageway – for example, when it's wet, how spray from other vehicles may affect visibility.

When can I use the right-hand lane?

On some dual carriageways, the lane on the right may be used for traffic turning right as well as for overtaking. If you're overtaking, watch for clues that traffic ahead of you is slowing down to turn right.

Can you overtake on the left-hand side of another vehicle?

You should not normally overtake on the left, but you can if the traffic is moving slowly in queues and the queue in the right-hand lane is moving more slowly.

Tips from the experts

If there's no slip road, join as you would on any other road.

If you're turning right onto a dual carriageway, you may treat it as 2 roads. When it's clear from the right, you may emerge and wait in the gap in the central reservation, as long as it's deep enough to protect your motorcycle. If it's not, you'll have to wait until the carriageway is clear in both directions before you join the carriageway.

When travelling on a dual carriageway at the national speed limit, remember that situations can change very quickly – use your mirrors frequently so that you always know what's happening around you.

What to expect on your module 2 test

If possible, your examiner will take you onto a road where the national speed limit applies, and watch to make sure that you join the road safely. Use your mirrors effectively and take account of the higher speed limit.

Recap questions

Q1 Which lane should you normally use when you're riding on a dual carriageway?

Q2 Why might a vehicle in the right-hand lane start slowing down or braking?

Reflection

Have you noticed how some dual carriageways have speed limits below the national speed limit? Why do you think that is? How will it affect you when you ride along one of these roads?

Weather conditions and road surfaces

Motorcyclists are particularly vulnerable to the effect of weather conditions, particularly wind, rain, snow and ice. You must be able to keep your visor (or goggles), mirrors and lights clean so that you always have a clear view of the road and other people can see you too. Rain, snow and ice also affect the road surface and there will be times when you should travel only if it's absolutely necessary.

Weather conditions you need to be able to cope with include

- **fog** – remember, fog is often patchy, so your visibility can change very quickly. Freezing fog has the added risk of icy road surfaces, ice on your visor and the rider becoming very cold, especially hands and feet
- **ice and snow** – check weather forecasts and make sensible decisions that minimise risk
- **bright sunshine** – be aware of the glare this may cause, especially when the road is wet or the sun is low
- **wind** – you'll be buffeted by gusts of wind around buildings, on bridges or other exposed stretches of road. For safety, some exposed routes may be closed to high-sided vehicles, cars towing caravans and motorcyclists
- **rain** – wet roads mean longer stopping distances. Your visibility may also be affected by spray from other vehicles.

You need to know

- the way that different weather conditions affect your visibility, stability, speed and stopping distance. You need to demonstrate that you can respond to these conditions safely
- your vehicle's features; for example, does it have fog lights or anti-lock brakes?
- the warning signs and signals that may be used
- how to reduce the likelihood of skidding and aquaplaning
- when to use your lights and which lights to use in poor daytime visibility.

Remember

When the roads are wet, your stopping distance may be doubled. In icy conditions, you may need to allow 10 times the normal stopping distance.

What if it becomes foggy?

Slow right down; it's much more difficult to judge distances and the speed of other vehicles in fog. Use dipped headlights and, if fitted, fog lights when visibility is seriously reduced.

What do I do if the road is flooded?

If the water is shallow, you may be able to ride through slowly. If you're not sure then do not ride into the flood. It might be too deep, the current may be strong, and there may be hidden obstacles under the water. If you do ride through flood water, remember to test your brakes afterwards.

Tips from the experts

Always keep your visor (or goggles), screen (if fitted) and mirrors clean and clear, so that you can see as much as possible all around.

High winds will affect you and some other road users, such as cyclists, drivers towing trailers or caravans and drivers of high-sided vehicles. Keep in mind that they may be blown into your path.

When visibility is reduced by fog, use dipped headlights and, if the distance you can see falls below 100 metres (328 feet), use your front and rear fog lights if you have them. If you do use fog lights, remember to switch them off when visibility improves.

It's not only bad weather that can cause difficult riding conditions. The glare of the sun – especially when the sun is low in the sky in winter – can make it very difficult to see other road users.

What to expect on your module 2 test

Your examiner will watch to see how you cope with the weather conditions prevailing during the test. You should know when it's necessary to use headlights and be capable of switching them on without prompting.

Recap questions

Q1 What are the main causes of skidding?

Q2 What should you do to keep good vision and visibility in bad weather?

Reflection

What weather conditions would make you postpone your journey? Are there alternative forms of transport that would get you to your destination with less risk?

Darkness

There are many factors that make riding in the dark more hazardous. Judging speed at night can be difficult, so be particularly careful at junctions.

You need to be confident riding on

- urban roads, where the variety of different lights, such as vehicle lights, street lights and shop signs, can be distracting
- rural roads, where the main source of light will be from vehicle headlights
- single and dual carriageways, where there may be a mixture of lighting.

You should know

- how darkness limits your visibility and therefore your speed, especially in bad weather
- when you need to use your lights, which lights to use and the importance of keeping them clean
- when you can use your horn at night
- how to park safely and legally when it's dark.

Remember
Even within the range of your lights, you cannot see as clearly as you would during daylight. Pedestrians, especially those wearing dark clothing, can be difficult to see.

What should I do if I'm following a slow-moving vehicle at night?

Before you overtake, you must make sure the road ahead is clear. There may be cyclists, pedestrians or obstructions in the road that are not lit. If you do overtake, do not dazzle the driver of the vehicle in front. Only switch your headlights onto main beam when you've passed the slow-moving vehicle.

What should I do if I'm dazzled by oncoming headlights?

Try not to look directly at the oncoming headlights – slow down and stop if it's necessary. Do not retaliate by leaving your headlights on full beam to dazzle the oncoming driver.

Tips from the experts

You should always ride so that you can stop safely within the distance you can see to be clear. At night, this means within the range of your lights.

Your lights are there to help you to be seen by others as well as to help you see. Make sure that you keep them clear and clean.

When following or meeting other vehicles, dip your headlights so that they do not dazzle other drivers.

Judging speed and distance at night can be difficult. Be particularly careful at junctions.

What to expect on your module 2 test

If conditions require it, your examiner will watch to make sure that you

- use your lights correctly
- ride so that you can stop safely within the distance you can see to be clear.

Recap questions

Q1 At night, when can you park on the side of the road without any lights?

Q1 When may you use your horn at night?

Reflection

Have you ever been dazzled by the headlights of an oncoming vehicle? What did you do? What might happen if you deliberately dazzle the driver of an oncoming vehicle?

Fuel-efficient riding

The type of motorcycle you ride, its engine size, fuel consumption and the way in which you ride, influence the local environment and ultimately the global climate. You need to understand how to minimise exhaust emissions through your riding behaviour. This benefits you by reducing your motorcycle's fuel consumption and improves your safety by developing your forward planning skills.

You need to understand how exhaust emissions affect the environment and be aware of

- the effect that vehicle exhaust gases have on the climate, your health, and the health and safety of others
- engine sizes. Motorcycles with bigger engines generally have higher fuel consumption and emissions than smaller ones
- how you can reduce fuel consumption by changing your riding style

- new technologies offering clean alternatives to fossil fuels.

To minimise your effect on the environment, you need to know how to

- reduce your fuel consumption by planning ahead and using the highest possible gear without making the engine struggle
- make sure your vehicle is serviced as per manufacturer's recommendations and is in a good condition
- check your tyres are at the correct pressure – low tyre pressure can have a significant effect on handling and fuel consumption
- dispose of vehicle waste, such as used engine oil, old batteries and tyres, correctly.

Remember

Many of the suggestions for reducing environmental impact will also reduce your motoring costs.

Does my speed really affect my fuel consumption?

Yes, it makes a big difference. At higher speeds, the engine has to do more work to overcome the air resistance. The harder your engine is working, the more fuel it's using.

Does the age of my motorcycle affect the level of exhaust emissions?

New motorcycles must meet the current standards and regulations. Generally, this makes them more fuel efficient than older models.

Tips from the experts

Ride smoothly. Use your hazard perception skills to plan ahead and avoid the need for heavy braking or brisk acceleration. Riding smoothly also reduces the wear and tear on your motorcycle.

Check tyre pressures regularly. Incorrect tyre pressure results in a shorter tyre life and may be dangerous. Under-inflated tyres can increase fuel consumption.

What to expect on your module 2 test

Your fuel-efficient riding style will be assessed during your on-road test. Any faults will be recorded, but they will not affect the result of your test. You'll also be asked questions that test your understanding of environmental issues during your theory test.

Recap question

Q1 How does engine size affect fuel consumption?

Reflection

What's stopping you changing your riding style to one that's more fuel efficient? Where could you find help to make the change?

Planning well ahead means you can control your speed in good time and often without needing to use the brakes.

Section three

The theory and practical tests

In this section, you'll learn about

- the theory test
  - multiple choice questions
  - hazard perception
  - on the day of your theory test
  - if you pass
  - if you fail
  - frequently asked questions
- the practical test
  - are you ready for your practical test?
  - on the day of your practical test
  - documents
  - the practical test: module 1
  - the practical test: module 2
- your test motorcycle
- booking your tests

The theory test

The theory test will gauge your knowledge and understanding of riding theory and hazard perception. A sound knowledge of the theory is essential to a better understanding of practical riding skills.

There are theory test centres across Great Britain and Northern Ireland. Theory test sessions are available on weekdays, some evenings and some Saturdays. You can find out where your local centre is from your trainer, online at **www.gov.uk** or by calling **0300 200 1122**.

There are 2 parts to the theory test: the first consists of multiple choice questions, and the second is a hazard perception test. You will take both parts in the same session.

Multiple choice questions

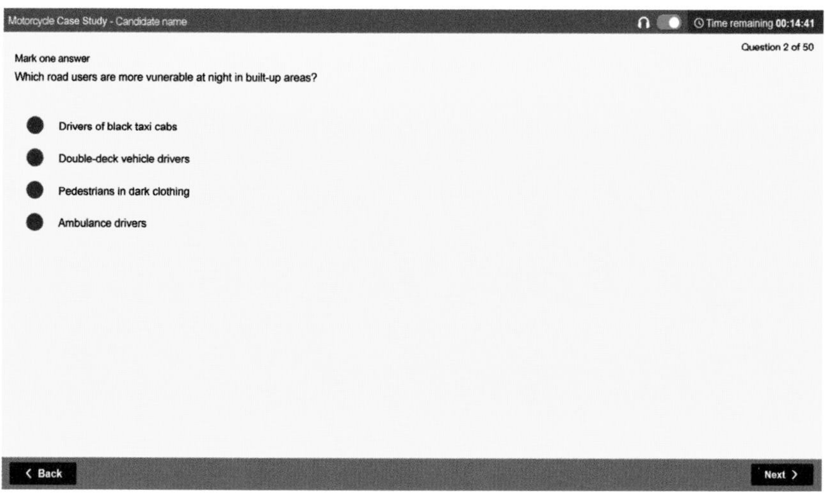

The first part of the theory test consists of 50 multiple choice questions. Some of the multiple choice questions will be presented as part of a case study. The questions will be on a screen and to answer a question, you click on the answer you think is correct. If you're not sure of the correct answer, you can flag the question and return to it later.

Take your time and read the questions carefully. You're given 57 minutes for this part of the test, so relax and do not rush. Some questions will take longer to answer than others, but there are no trick questions. The time remaining is displayed on the screen.

Try to answer all the questions. If you're well prepared, you should not find them difficult.

At the end of this part of the test, you can use the 'review' feature to check your answers. If you click the 'review' button and then the 'end' button on the review screen, it will end your test.

Hazard perception

After you've finished the multiple choice questions, there's a break of up to 3 minutes before you start the hazard perception part of the test. You cannot leave your seat during this break. This part of the test is a series of CGI video clips, shown from a driver/rider's point of view. You'll be using a mouse for this part of the theory test.

Before you start this part of the test, you'll be shown a short CGI video that explains how the test works and gives you a chance to see a sample clip. This will help you to understand what you need to do. You can play this video again if you wish.

During the hazard perception part of the test, you'll be shown 14 CGI video clips. Each clip contains one or more developing hazards. You should press the mouse button as soon as you see a hazard developing that may need you to take some action, such as changing speed or direction. The earlier you notice a developing hazard and make a response, the higher your score. There are 15 hazards for which you can score points.

The hazard perception part of the test lasts about 20 minutes. For this part of the test, no extra time is available, and you cannot repeat any of the clips – you do not get a second chance to see a hazard when you're riding on the road.

We strongly recommend that you use the official DVSA hazard perception training materials, preferably with your trainer, to prepare for the hazard perception part of the theory test.

Visit the DVSA eLearning site at **www.safedrivingforlife.info**, where you will find online hazard perception training. There's an app too if you prefer your training that way.

On the day of your theory test

The test centre staff will check your documents. You'll have to show your driving licence and, if your licence does not show your photograph, you'll also have to show your passport (your passport does not have to be British). No other form of identification is acceptable in England, Wales or Scotland.

Other forms of identification may be acceptable in Northern Ireland. Please check **nidirect.gov.uk/motoring** or refer to your test appointment email or letter. All documents must be original. We cannot accept photocopies.

Arrive in plenty of time so that you're not rushed. If you arrive late, you may not be allowed to take the test.

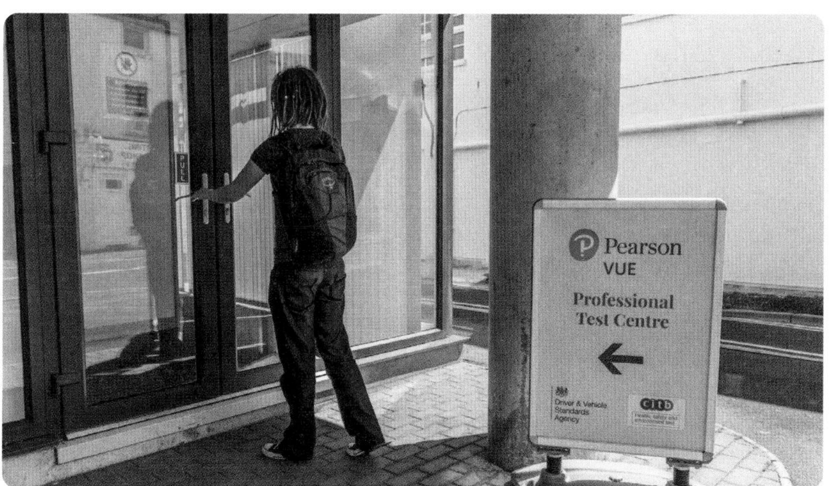

If you pass

The result should be available within 10 minutes of completing your test. When you pass your theory test, you'll be given a pass certificate. You have to quote the number on this certificate when you book a practical test, and you must bring the certificate with you when you take your practical test.

Your theory test pass certificate is valid for 2 years and you must take it with you when you go for your practical tests. You must take and pass both practical test modules before your theory test pass certificate expires or you'll have to take the theory test again plus both modules of the practical test to gain a full licence.

If you fail

If you have not passed the theory test, then you must retake it. You'll have to wait a minimum of 3 clear working days before you take the test again.

Frequently asked questions

Do I need to take the theory test?

All motorcycle test candidates will have to pass the theory test before a booking for a practical test will be accepted. However, you will not have to take a theory test if you want to take an A1 small motorcycle test and hold a full moped licence obtained by passing both a theory and practical moped test or if you're upgrading your motorcycle licence from an A1 to A2 or A2 to A under the progressive access rules.

If you want to take a practical motorcycle test under the direct access rules then you need a valid motorcycle theory test pass certificate.

How do I know that I'm ready for the theory test?

If you're well prepared, you should not find the questions difficult. 'The Official DVSA Theory Test for Motorcyclists' is available as a book, an eBook or eLearning and it contains comprehensive information about the test and all the revision questions, answers and explanations.

You should also study your copy of 'The Highway Code' and the publications 'The Official DVSA Guide to Riding – the essential skills' and 'Know Your Traffic Signs'. Always make sure that you have the most up-to-date versions of these books.

It's very important that you know and understand why the answers to the multiple choice questions are correct. Take this knowledge and put it into practice on the road. Your examiner will expect you to demonstrate what you've learned through your riding.

I cannot read very well, so I'm worried about taking my test

If you have reading difficulties, there's a voiceover for the test, which may help. You may also be allowed extra time in some circumstances (see pages 30 to 31). You can select this option when you book your test online.

How will I know what to do on the hazard perception part of the test?

Once you've completed the multiple choice part of the test, and before you start the hazard perception part, you'll be shown a short tutorial video that explains how the test works and gives you a chance to see a sample clip. This will help you to understand what you're expected to do once the second part of the test starts.

Why do I have to retake both parts of the test if I only fail one?

It's really only one test. The theory test has always included questions relating to hazard awareness – the second part simply tests the same skills in a more effective way. The 2 parts are only presented separately in the theory test because different scoring methods are used.

What's the pass mark?

To pass the multiple choice part of the theory test, you must answer at least 43 out of 50 questions correctly. For learner car drivers and motorcyclists, the pass mark for the hazard perception part is 44 out of 75.

If I do not pass, when can I take the test again?

If you fail your test, you've shown that you're not fully prepared. You'll have to wait at least 3 clear working days before you can take the theory test again.

Good preparation will save you both time and money.

The practical test

Are you ready for your practical test?

If you've taken additional training, be guided by your trainer, who has the knowledge and experience to tell you when you're ready for each module.

For module 1, you should be able to complete the manoeuvres consistently well, while for module 2, you must be able to ride with confidence and without assistance or guidance from your trainer.

If you cannot do this yet, waiting until you're ready will save you time and money.

On the day of your practical test

Make sure that you arrive for your test in good time and try to relax. You need to bring the correct documents with you and ensure that the motorcycle you'll be riding is suitable for the category of test you're taking. Your examiner will be understanding and sympathetic and will make every effort to put you at ease. At the beginning of the test your examiner will ask you to

- sign a residency and insurance declaration
- show your documents.

Documents

When you arrive at the test centre, you need to have with you your

- driving licence. If your licence does not show your photograph you'll need your valid passport. (Your passport does not have to be British.) No other form of identification is acceptable in England, Wales or Scotland. Other documents may, however, be acceptable in Northern Ireland; please check **nidirect.gov.uk/motoring**
- theory test pass certificate (unless you're upgrading your licence under progressive access)
- CBT completion certificate (unless you're upgrading your licence under progressive access).

For the module 2 test, you need your module 1 pass certificate.

All documents must be original. DVSA cannot accept photocopies.

The practical test

The practical test is split into 2 separate modules – module 1, an off-road module, and module 2, an on-road module. You must

- pass module 1 before you can take module 2
- pass both modules within 2 years of passing your theory test. Different rules apply under progressive access; see pages 22 and 23
- hold a current CBT completion certificate when taking both modules unless you're upgrading a full motorcycle licence in a lower category
- use the same category of motorcycle for modules 1 and 2.

Module 1 is an off-road, specified manoeuvring test including an avoidance exercise, a U-turn, a slow ride and a controlled stop (see section 4). This will take place on the off-road manoeuvring area at the test centre.

Module 2 is a road riding test that starts and finishes at the test centre. See section 5.

Your test motorcycle

There are 3 categories of motorcycle licence (see page 21). The table below explains the test vehicle requirements to obtain them.

Category	Test vehicle requirements
A1	Motorcycle • with a cubic capacity of between 120 cc and 125 cc • with a power output of up to 11 kW (14.6 bhp) • capable of a speed of at least 90 km/h (55 mph).
A2	Motorcycle • with a cubic capacity of at least 395 cc* • with a power output of between 20 kW and 35 kW (between 26.8 bhp and 46.6 bhp) • with a power-to-weight ratio not exceeding 0.2 kW/kg • that, if restricted, is not derived from a machine more than double its original power.
A	Motorcycle • with a cubic capacity of at least 595 cc • an engine power of at least 50 kW (67 bhp) • a minimum kerb weight of 180 kg.

Important You must use the same category of motorcycle for both practical test modules.

Your machine must

- have a current test certificate, if it's over the prescribed age.
- be fully covered by insurance for you to ride on the date of your test and for its present use.
- have the correct engine size/power output for the category of test that you're taking (see table above).
- be properly taxed or licensed.
- have red L plates (or D plates in Wales) fitted that must be visible from the front and rear.

*At the time of going to print, the minimum test vehicle engine size for category A2 is under review. Please visit **www.gov.uk** for the most up-to-date information.

If you overlook any of these, your test may be cancelled, and you could lose your fee.

Mopeds Any motorcycle with an engine smaller than 50 cc is classed as a moped. If you pass your test on a moped, you'll gain a category P licence.

Booking your tests

Some approved training bodies (ATBs) will be able to book your theory and practical tests for you. Alternatively, you can book your tests online or by telephone, as explained below.

Booking online or by telephone

You can book theory and practical tests by either of these methods and you'll be given the date and time of your test immediately.

You can book online at **www.gov.uk**

To book by telephone, call **0300 200 1122**. If you're a Welsh speaker call **0300 200 1133**. If you have hearing or speech difficulties and use a minicom machine call **0300 200 1166** for theory tests and **0300 200 1144** for practical tests.

To book in Northern Ireland, call **0845 600 6700** for theory tests and **0870 247 2472** for practical tests.

When booking, you'll need to identify what sort of test you want to book and provide

- your driver number (from your licence)
- credit or debit card details. Please note that the person who books the test must be the card holder
- if you're booking a practical test, you'll need your theory test pass certificate number (unless you're exempt).

Appointment confirmation

Your confirmation will be sent in the post if you do not provide an email address.

Disabilities or special needs

Whichever test you book, you need to let them know if you have a disability or if there are any other special circumstances. You'll still take the same type of test as every other test candidate, but more time may be allowed for the test.

To make sure enough time is allowed, it would help DVSA to know if you

- are deaf or have severe hearing difficulties
- are in any way restricted in your movements
- have any disability that may affect your riding.

If you're deaf or have severe hearing difficulties, you're allowed to bring a signer (this can be your trainer if you wish). The signer must be 16 years or over.

You must take the test in English, Welsh or British Sign Language. You cannot bring a foreign language interpreter with you on your motorcycle test.

There are some different procedures for theory tests in Northern Ireland - see **nidirect.gov.uk**

How much do the tests cost?

Your ATB should be able to tell you or you can find out from **www.gov.uk** or by calling **0300 200 1122**.

Can I take my tests on a weekend or in the evening?

Theory tests are available on some weekday evenings and Saturdays. Practical tests are available at some test centres on Saturdays, Sundays and, in the summer, on weekday evenings. The fee for practical tests taken outside normal working hours is higher than during normal working hours on weekdays.

How do I change or cancel my test appointment?

You can change or cancel your test appointment online at **www.gov.uk**. Alternatively, you can change or cancel a test appointment by calling **0300 200 1122**.

You need to give at least 3 clear working days' notice for changes to or cancellation of a theory test or practical module, not counting the day DVSA receive your request and the day of the test (Saturday is counted as a working day). If you do not give enough notice, you'll lose your fee.

Section four

Module 1

The off-road practical riding test

In this section, you'll learn about

- the off-road module
- the off-road manoeuvring area
- the module 1 exercises
- other machines.

The off-road module

You need to successfully complete the off-road module of the practical motorcycle test (module 1) before you can take the accompanied on-road module (module 2).

Module 1 will last about 20 minutes.

At the beginning of the test, your examiner will ask you to

- sign an insurance and residency declaration
- show your documents (see page 127).

You'll then be asked to ride your motorcycle onto the motorcycle manoeuvring area. When you're on the area, behave as if you're riding on the public road. You should include any necessary safety checks, and you should avoid riding into any of the marker cones.

Your examiner will ask you to push or ride your motorcycle forwards into one of the bays formed by marker cones and put it on its stand.

The module 1 exercises

The off-road module includes

- using the stand
- manual handling
- slalom and figure of 8
- slow ride
- U-turn
- cornering with a controlled stop
- cornering with an emergency stop
- cornering with an avoidance exercise.

Your examiner will explain each exercise to you using a diagram (see page 135) to describe the requirements. If you commit a serious or dangerous fault during the off-road element, you will not pass the test.

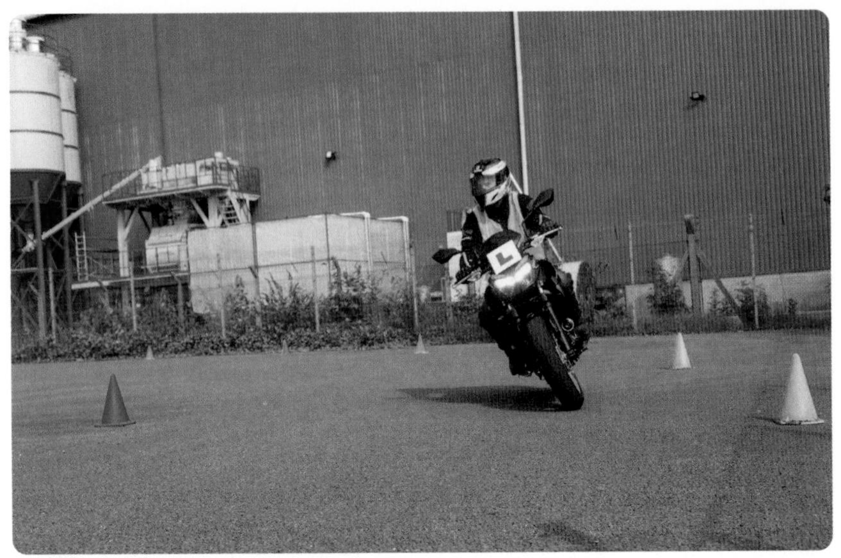

How your module 1 test is assessed

Your examiner will make a note of

- **dangerous faults** – these involve actual danger to you, the examiner, the public or property
- **serious faults** – these are potentially dangerous
- **riding faults** – these are not potentially dangerous, but could become serious if you keep making the same mistake.

You'll pass module 1 if you make

- no serious or dangerous faults (sometimes called 'majors')
- no more than 5 riding faults (sometimes called 'minors').

If you pass module 1, you'll be given a module 1 pass certificate. This will show the category of motorcycle you used. Keep it safe, as you'll have to show it to your examiner when you attend for module 2.

The off-road manoeuvring are

Left circuit (the right circuit mirrors this layout)

Key

1 Stands and manual handling
2 Slalom
3 Figure of 8
4 Slow ride
5 U-turn
6 Cornering
7 Controlled stop
8 30 km/h (19 mph) circuit ride
9 50 km/h (32 mph) emergency brake
10 30 km/h (19 mph) circuit ride
11 50 km/h (32 mph) avoidance

Mopeds

For all mopeds, speed requirements are 30 kph/19 mph.

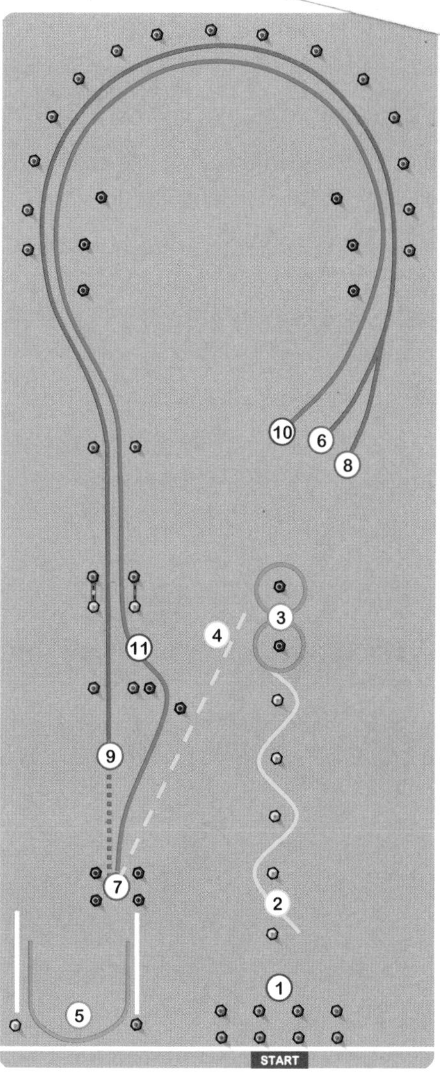

Diagram for illustrative purposes only. For details of the circuit measurements, see the information about the motorcycle practical riding test at **www.gov.uk**
Please note: at certain sites and in Northern Ireland, the circuit layout may vary in shape, although the manoeuvres are the same. For further details, please speak to your trainer or visit **www.gov.uk**. For Northern Ireland, visit **nidirect.gov.uk/motoring**

Before you start the engine

What the test requires

You must check that

- the fuel tap is turned on
- the engine kill switch is in the 'on' position
- the gear lever is in neutral.

If your motorcycle has an inhibitor switch that prevents it from being ridden with the stand down, you must know the correct procedures to deal with this safety feature.

Remember

If the fuel tap is in the reserve position instead of the 'on' position, the motorcycle will run normally but there will be no warning when your fuel is running low.

Using the stand and manual handling

What the test requires

You'll need to show that you can take the motorcycle off the stand and wheel it backwards from one bay to another without using the engine. You may choose to wheel it backwards in an arc from one bay to the other, or you may choose to wheel it backwards out of the first bay before pushing it forwards and then backwards into the next bay.

When you've wheeled it into the next bay, you'll need to put it back on its stand. You may use either the side or the centre stand.

How your examiner will test you

When taking your motorcycle off its stand or when wheeling it, you must

- make any necessary safety checks
- keep your balance
- keep control of the motorcycle
- position the motorcycle accurately
- avoid touching the marker cones
- set the stand correctly.

Paddling or sitting astride the machine to move it is not allowed other than by candidates with disabilities or other special circumstances, such as

- limited mobility
- restricted leg movement.

Remember
A motorcycle without a stand is not suitable for the test.

Slalom and figure of 8

What the test requires

You'll be asked to ride a slalom and a figure of 8. This is to demonstrate your ability to ride and steer your motorcycle slowly, and under control, while manoeuvring in a restricted space.

How your examiner will test you

You'll need to make effective safety checks before starting. Your examiner will look for skilled use of the

- throttle
- clutch
- rear brake

so that you can

- steer accurately between the marker cones
- keep your balance at the low speed necessary to complete the exercise.

The slalom exercise will lead into 2 circuits of the figure of 8.

Tip

You should maintain a reasonable degree of slow-speed control and balance throughout the exercise.

Slow ride

What the test requires

You'll be asked to demonstrate your ability to ride slowly, in a straight line, as if in slow-moving traffic.

How your examiner will test you

You should make effective safety checks before you move away. Your examiner will look for skilled use of the throttle, clutch and rear brake so that you can

- ride slowly
- ride in a reasonably straight line.

Remember

You need to be able to stay in control of your machine while you're riding slowly.

U-turn

What the test requires

You'll be asked to ride a U-turn between 2 lines representing either side of a public road.

How your examiner will test you

You'll need to make effective safety checks before you move away and before you turn.

Your examiner will look for skilled use of the throttle, clutch and rear brake so that you can

- turn your machine round under control and accurately between the lines
- keep your balance.

Cornering and controlled stopping

What the test requires

Your examiner will ask you to ride a left or a right circuit. You will need to control your motorcycle safely and then bring it to a controlled stop in an area formed by marker cones.

How your examiner will test you

You'll need to make effective safety checks before starting the exercise. Your examiner will look for skilled use of the controls so that you can

- enter, ride around and leave the bend under control
- bring your machine to a stop accurately and under full control
- stop within the area formed by marker cones.

Tip

There's no minimum speed requirement for this exercise, but you'll be asked to try to reach a speed of 30 to 50 km/h (20 to 30 mph) as you pass the speed measuring equipment.

Cornering and the emergency stop

What the test requires

You'll need to demonstrate your ability to stop as quickly and safely as possible while staying in full control of your motorcycle.

Your examiner will ask you to ride a left or a right circuit. If you reach a speed of around 30 km/h (about 19 mph) while riding round the bend, it will help you reach the minimum speed required of 50 km/h (about 32 mph) as you pass the speed measuring device.

Soon after you pass the speed measuring device, your examiner will give you a signal to stop, as in an emergency. They will show you what the signal is before you begin.

How your examiner will test you

You'll need to make effective safety checks before starting the exercise. Your examiner will look for skilled use of the

- throttle
- clutch
- gears
- front and rear brakes

so that you can

- enter and leave the bend under control and with accuracy
- respond quickly to the signal to stop given by the examiner
- apply maximum braking and bring your machine to a stop under full control, without skidding.

Tip

The speed measuring device will record your speed before the emergency stop. If you ride too slowly and do not achieve the minimum speed requirement, your examiner may allow you to repeat the exercise.

If you commit a serious or dangerous fault during this exercise, you will not be asked to carry out the avoidance exercise.

Cornering and the avoidance exercise

What the test requires

Your examiner will ask you to ride a left or a right circuit. If you reach a speed of around 30 km/h (about 19 mph) while riding round the bend, it will help you reach the minimum speed required of 50 km/h (about 32 mph) as you pass the speed measuring device.

When you've passed the speed measuring device, you'll need to control your motorcycle safely while steering to avoid a stationary obstacle. You'll then need to bring it to a controlled stop in an area formed by marker cones.

How your examiner will test you

You should make effective safety checks before starting the exercise. Your examiner will look for skilled use of the

- throttle
- clutch
- gears
- front brake
- rear brake

so that you can

- enter and leave the bend under control and with accuracy
- meet the minimum speed requirement before avoiding an obstacle
- steer accurately between marker cones
- bring your motorcycle safely to a controlled halt within the marker cones.

The speed measuring device will accurately record your speed before you carry out the avoidance exercise.

Tip

If you ride too slowly and do not achieve the minimum speed requirement, your examiner may allow you to repeat the exercise.

Other machines

Mopeds

If you take your test on a moped, the minimum speed for the left or right circuit ride, avoidance and emergency stop exercises will be 30 km/h (about 19 mph). All other aspects of the test are the same.

Combination sidecars

You can take your test on a motorcycle with a sidecar only if you have a physical disability.

You will not need to do the

- exercise using the stand
- wheeling exercises
- avoidance exercise.

You will be allowed extra time for your test.

If the sidecar is on the left of the machine, your examiner will ask you to ride a right circuit. If the sidecar is on the right of the machine, your examiner will ask you to ride a left circuit.

Your examiner will adjust the slalom marker cones to allow for the extra width of the vehicle. The width between the cones associated with the speed measuring device and the controlled stopping box will be increased to 1.5 times the width of the vehicle.

Your examiner can ask you to do the U-turn exercise from either left right or right to left.

Section five

Module 2

The on-road practical riding test

In this section, you'll learn about

- the on-road module
- the eyesight test
- safety checks and balance questions
- stopping and moving away safely
- independent riding
- your test result
- the enhanced rider scheme.

The on-road module

You must pass both the off-road and on-road modules within 2 years of passing your theory test. Different rules apply under progressive access (see pages 122 and 123). In addition, you must hold a current CBT completion certificate when taking both modules unless you're upgrading a full motorcycle licence in a lower category.

Your examiner will be understanding and sympathetic and will make every effort to put you at ease.

At the beginning of the on-road module, your examiner will ask you to

- sign an insurance and residency declaration
- show your documents (see page 127).

You'll then be fitted with a radio system. Your examiner will explain how directions will be given and check that the radio equipment is working. The radio allows you to hear your examiner, but you will not be able to talk to them over the radio.

The test has many elements, including

- eyesight test
- answering safety check and balance questions
- riding independently
- stopping and moving away safely.

Your riding should show that you've fully understood everything that you learned for the theory test. You should show

- you have good control of your motorcycle
- courtesy and consideration to other road users
- awareness of stopping distances, speed limits and safety margins in all conditions
- hazard awareness
- correct action concerning pedestrians and other vulnerable road users
- you can deal safely with other types of vehicles
- you understand road and traffic signs.

How your module 2 test is assessed

Your examiner is looking for evidence that you have the required skills, knowledge, and attitude to be safe on the road.

Throughout your module 2 test, your examiner will assess your riding and will make a note of any faults you make. You'll fail your test if you commit a serious or dangerous fault. You'll also fail if you commit more than 10 riding faults.

Your examiner will use the following criteria

- **Riding fault** Less serious, but has been assessed as such because of circumstances at that particular time. An accumulation of more than 10 riding faults will result in a fail.
- **Serious fault** Recorded when your riding has caused something potentially dangerous, or a habitual riding fault indicates a serious weakness in your riding.
- **Dangerous fault** Recorded when a fault is assessed as having caused actual danger.

At the end of the test, you'll be offered some general guidance to explain your riding test report.

When you pass both modules

When you've passed both modules, you'll be allowed to ride without L plates, unsupervised and on motorways. The category of motorcycle you'll be licensed to ride immediately after passing both modules will depend on the machine you've used. See Your test motorcycle on page 128.

How long will module 2 last?

Module 2 will last about 35 to 40 minutes.

Are examiners supervised?

Examiners are frequently supervised by a senior officer. If a senior officer is present at your test, do not worry. They're only there to check that your examiner is testing you properly and will not interfere with the test or the result. They're not there to test you in any way.

Does the standard of the test vary?

No. All examiners are trained to carry out tests to the same standard. Test routes are as uniform as possible and include a range of typical road and traffic conditions.

Where can I find a guide to what happens during the modules?

Watch Motorcycle test 2021 – module 1
youtube.com/watch?v=G3bVhFzTMHo

and module 2
youtube.com/watch?v=gIUw46kkEzk

Can anyone accompany me on my test?

Your trainer may be able to accompany you on your test. You should ask your examiner about this. If you're deaf or have severe hearing difficulties, you're allowed to bring a signer; this can be your trainer.

The Data Protection Act prevents your trainer from talking to your examiner about your practical test without your permission. If you did not pass your test and want your trainer to help you understand the reason(s) why, your trainer needs to be on hand at the end of the test to listen to the debrief that the examiner will offer you. Tell the examiner that you would like your trainer to be present. This can help your trainer to plan any further training that you might need.

The eyesight test

In good daylight, you **MUST** be able to read a clean vehicle number plate from 20 metres (about 66 feet). If you need glasses or contact lenses to read the number plate, that's fine. However, you **MUST** wear them during the test and whenever you ride.

If you've had sight correction surgery, you should declare this when you apply for your provisional licence.

How will my examiner check my eyesight?

Before you begin riding, your examiner will point out a vehicle and ask you to read its number plate.

If you have difficulty reading, you may copy down what you see.

If you cannot read that number plate, your examiner will find another vehicle and measure the exact distance and repeat the test.

If you cannot demonstrate to your examiner that your eyesight meets the required standard

- you will have failed your motorcycle test
- your test will go no further.

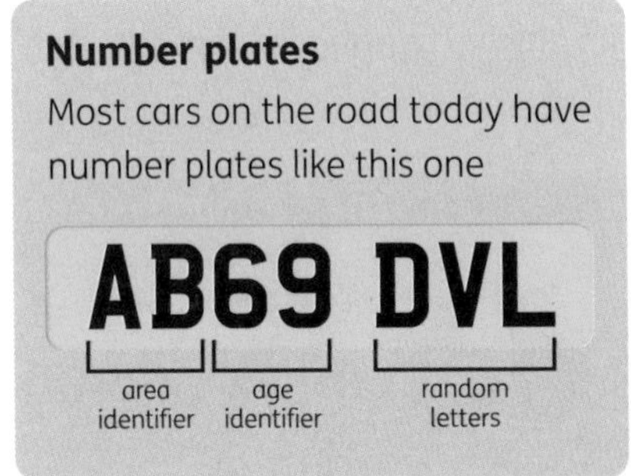

Number plates
Most cars on the road today have number plates like this one
AB69 DVL
area identifier
age identifier
random letters

Safety check and balance questions

The examiner wants to see that you're familiar with the motorcycle you're using for the test and that you can prepare to ride it safely by carrying out basic safety checks.

You'll be expected to know how to carry out checks relating to

- tyres
- brakes
- fluids
- lights
- reflectors
- direction indicators
- horn.

You must also know how balance will be affected when carrying a pillion passenger.

What kind of safety questions will I be asked?

At the start of the test, your examiner will ask you 2 safety check questions to test your knowledge and understanding of basic vehicle safety (see the annex).

You will not be asked to touch a hot engine or physically check the fluid levels.

In addition, your examiner will ask you one question about balance when carrying a pillion passenger. This will not be complicated; for example: 'How would the balance of the motorcycle be affected if you carried a pillion passenger?'

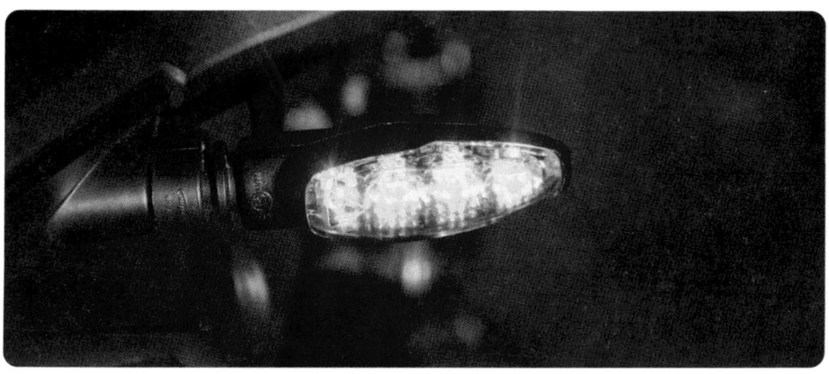

Stopping and moving away safely

Your examiner will ask you to pull up on the left several times during the test. This is to demonstrate your ability to stop and move away

- safely
- on a gradient
- from behind a parked vehicle.

You should be able to select a place to stop where

- you will not obstruct the road
- you do not create a hazard
- you're allowed to stop.

When stopping, you should

- use the OSM/PSL routine
- show good judgement and planning
- give a signal if necessary
- pull up close to the edge of the road.

When you move away on the level or on a gradient, you should use your mirrors, show good control of your motorcycle and remember to check your blind area before moving away.

Why will I need to move away from behind a parked vehicle?

When you move away from behind a parked vehicle, you will need to use the same skills as you would moving away on the level or on a gradient. In addition, you'll need

- good control as you steer sharply around the parked vehicle
- to make sure you do not ride out into the path of other traffic.

Your examiner wants to see you have the skill and ability to perform this exercise safely.

Independent riding

This part of the test will last around 10 minutes.

Your examiner will ask you to pull up and will then explain the exercise. You'll be asked to ride following traffic signs to a destination, or follow a series of verbal directions, or a combination of both.

It will not matter if you go the wrong way unless, in doing so, you make a riding fault.

You'll need to plan ahead because your examiner will not be prompting you by giving you directions over the radio.

To ride independently and keep full control, you need to

- plan ahead so that you do not have to make any late decisions
- be able to follow verbal directions and traffic signs
- use the OSM/PSL routine (see pages 79 to 80)
- give signals correctly and in good time but not too early or you may mislead other road users, especially if there's another turning before your junction
- take up the correct position on the road
- understand the correct use of lanes, both with and without directional information
- respond correctly to other road users
- know and respond to traffic signs, signals and road markings.

What should I do if I take a wrong turning?

If you realise you're taking the wrong turning, do not make a sudden change of direction, as this could cause a collision. It's better to complete the turn safely and then find somewhere safe to turn around and rejoin your route.

Your test result

If you do not pass

Your riding is not up to the standard required. You've made

- serious or dangerous faults
- more than the fixed number of riding faults allowed.

Your examiner will help you by

- giving you a copy of the riding test report. This will show all the faults recorded during the test
- explaining briefly why you have not passed.

Listen to your examiner carefully. They'll be able to help you by pointing out the aspects of your riding that you need to improve. If you wish, your trainer may be present while your examiner explains why you have not passed.

Study the riding test report. It will include notes to help you understand how the examiner records faults. You may then find it helpful to refer to the relevant sections in this book.

If your trainer is not present during your examiner's explanation, you should show them your copy of the test report. Your trainer will advise and help you to correct the faults. Listen to their advice carefully and get as much practice as you can.

Right of appeal

You'll obviously be disappointed if you do not pass either module. Although your examiner's decision cannot be changed, if you think your test was not carried out according to the regulations, you have the right to appeal.

If you live in England and Wales, you have 6 months after the issue of the Statement of Failure in which to appeal (Magistrates' Courts Act 1952 Ch. 55 part VII, Sect. 104).

If you live in Scotland, you have 21 days in which to appeal (Sheriff Court, Scotland Act of Sederunt (Statutory Appeals) 1981).

If you pass

Well done! You'll have shown that you can ride safely and confidently.

At the end of module 2, your examiner will give you a copy of the riding test report. This will show any riding faults that have been recorded during the test and some notes to explain them.

Your examiner will ask for your driving licence so that an upgraded licence can automatically be sent to you through the post. You'll be given a pass certificate (DSA10) as proof of success, until you receive your new full licence.

If you do not want to surrender your licence, you do not have to, and there will be certain circumstances when this is not possible; for example, if you've changed your name or address.

In these cases, you'll have to send your provisional licence together with your pass certificate and the appropriate fee to DVLA, and they'll send you your full licence. You must do this within 2 years, or you'll have to take your test again.

You can also talk to your trainer about further training and the enhanced rider scheme - see page 156.

Fuel-efficient riding

Fuel-efficient riding is a style of riding that contributes to road safety while reducing fuel consumption and emissions.

At the end of the test, the examiner may remind you to discuss fuel-efficient riding with your trainer and the benefits it brings.

The enhanced rider scheme

DVSA, in partnership with training experts and leading insurance companies, has developed a package of training known as the DVSA enhanced rider scheme.

The scheme is intended to benefit all motorcycle riders who have a full motorcycle licence, irrespective of riding experience, including those who have just passed their test. Those who undertake further rider development under the scheme will receive considerable insurance discounts from the insurance companies that have signed up to the scheme.

Trainers who deliver the DVSA enhanced rider scheme must be registered with DVSA as a DVSA enhanced rider scheme trainer.

To find out more about the DVSA enhanced rider scheme, or to look for a trainer in your area, visit **www.gov.uk**

Section six

Retesting

In this section, you'll learn about

- the New Drivers Act
- the extended test
- applying for a retest.

The New Drivers Act

Special rules apply for the first 2 years after the date of passing your first practical test if you held nothing but a provisional licence before passing your test.

How you may be affected

Your licence will be revoked if the number of penalty points on your licence reaches 6 or more because of offences you commit before the 2 years are over. This includes offences that you committed before passing your test.

You must then apply for a provisional licence and complete CBT before riding on the road. You may ride only as a learner until you pass the theory and both modules of the practical test again.

This applies even if you pay by fixed penalty.

For more information, see **www.gov.uk**

The extended test

Tough penalties exist for anyone convicted of dangerous driving or riding offences.

Courts must impose an extended test on anyone convicted of such offences.

Courts can also

- impose an extended driving or riding test on anyone convicted of other offences involving obligatory disqualification
- order a normal-length test for other endorsable offences before the disqualified driver or rider can recover a full licence.

Applying for a retest

If you need to be retested, you can apply for a provisional licence at the end of the disqualification period. You must complete CBT before riding on the road.

The normal rules for provisional licence holders apply

- red L plates (or, if you wish, D plates in Wales) must be displayed to the front and rear of the machine
- solo motorcycles must not exceed 125 cc and 11 kW power output (unless you're riding under the direct or progressive access scheme)
- riding on motorways is not allowed
- pillion passengers may not be carried.

You can book an extended test in the same way as a normal test (see pages 130 to 131).

The theory test

You'll have to pass the theory test before you can apply for the practical test.

Details of the theory test can be found in section 3.

Longer and more demanding

The extended test takes about 70 minutes and covers a wide variety of roads, usually including dual carriageways. The extended test is assessed to the same standard as the learner test but is more demanding due to the longer time devoted to normal riding.

You're advised to take suitable instruction from an approved motorcycle trainer before taking this test.

Higher fee

The higher fee reflects the longer duration of the test.

How your examiner will test you

Your test will include all off-road and on-road exercises included in the normal test. Your examiner will watch you and take account of

- your ability to concentrate for the duration of the test
- your attitude towards other road users.

Annex

Official motorcycle safety questions

'Tell me' questions

1. **Identify where you would check the engine oil level and tell me how you would check that the engine has sufficient oil.**

   Identify where to check level, i.e. dipstick or sight glass. Explain that level should be between max and min marks. For dipstick remove dipstick and wipe clean, return and remove again to check oil level against max/min marks. For sight glass, ensure glass is clean when checking.

2. **Show me how you would check that the horn is working on this machine (off road only).**

   Check is carried out by using control (turn on ignition if necessary).

3. **Identify where the brake fluid reservoir is and tell me how you would check that you have a safe level of hydraulic fluid.**

   Identify reservoir, check level against high/low markings.

4. **Tell me how you would check that the lights and reflectors are clean and working.**

   Explanation only: Operate switch (turn on ignition if necessary), identify reflectors. Check visually for cleanliness and operation.

5. **Show me how you would check that the brake lights are working.**

   Operate brake, place hand over light or make use of reflections in windows, garage doors etc, or ask someone to help.

6. **Tell me how you would check the condition of the chain on this machine.**

   Check for chain wear, correct tension and rear wheel alignment. Tension should be adjusted as specified in the machine handbook. Drive chain should be lubricated to ensure that excessive wear does not take place.

7. **Show me what checks you would make on the steering movement before using the machine.**

   Handlebars should be free to move smoothly from full left lock to full right lock without any control cables being stretched, trapped or pinched and without any snagging between moving and fixed parts.

8. **Tell me how you would check your tyres to ensure that they are correctly inflated, have sufficient tread depth and that their general condition is safe to use on the road.**

   Correct tyre pressure settings can be found in the owner's manual. Pressures should be checked using a reliable gauge. Tread depth must be at least 1mm deep, forming a continuous band at least 3/4 of the breadth of the tread and all the way around. There should be no lumps, bulges or tears.

9. **Show me how you would check the operation of the front brake on this machine.**

   Wheel the machine forward and apply the front brake.

10. **Show me how you would check the operation of the brakes on this machine.**

    Check for excessive travel on the brake lever and the brake pedal and for unusual play or sponginess.

11. **Show me how you would check the operation of the engine cut-out switch.**

    Operate switch, without the engine being started.

12. **Show me how you would switch on the rear fog light and explain when you would use it (if fitted).**

    Operate switch (turn on ignition and dipped headlights if necessary). Check warning light is on. Explain use.

13. **Show me how you switch your headlights from dipped to main beam.**

    Operate switch (with ignition or engine on if necessary). Check with main beam warning light.